NO-HITTER

NO-HITTER

Phil Pepe

FOUR WINDS PRESS · NEW YORK

Photo Credits:

Malcolm W. Emmons, pp. 27, 28, 47 (bottom)
Ken Regan, front cover, p. 47 (top)
UPI, all other inside photographs

Second printing, 1968

Published by Four Winds Press
A Division of Scholastic Magazines, Inc., New York, N.Y.
By Arrangement with Associated Features Inc.
Copyright © 1968 by Associated Features Inc.
All rights reserved.
Printed in the United States of America.
Library of Congress Catalogue Card Number: 68–12389

FOREWORD

My brother Paul and I had come home from watching our Dodgers play as we had done so many times in those gay, carefree days of our youth. But this day was unlike any of the others. This day was something special.

It was April 23, 1946, and, wonder of wonders, we had watched Ed Head pitch a no-hitter against the Boston Braves.

We were a couple of excited kids. Into the night we talked about the spectacle and about the good fortune that permitted us to be there because school was out that week. We talked about it so much that Mom, who never knew second base from the bullpen, but who always took an interest in her boys, asked, "Who hit the no-hitter?"

Perhaps that was when this book actually was born. So this is a book for my mom and for all the moms like her — and especially for Jayne, David, and Jimmy's mom.

My mom always thought I spent too much time with baseball and not enough with arithmetic, and this book is for her because she recognized that was the way it had to be. Look Ma, a book on baseball! I could never have written one on arithmetic.

This book is also for my dad, who discovered baseball later in his life. Too bad. He became a Giant fan. We always figured he was too old to know better.

Finally, a special word of thanks to Zander Hollander for his great guidance, then and now. Without him, none of this would have been possible.

Phil Pepe
January 1, 1968

Glen Rock, New Jersey

CONTENTS

INTRODUCTION 9
SANDY 15
GEORGE WASHINGTON PITCHED HERE . . 35
TWO OF A KIND 43
BACK TO BACK 65
BUMPER CROP 78
ONCE IN A LIFETIME 95
ODDLY ENOUGH 122
THE LOSERS 133
BO AND DOUBLE BO 146
HEX MARKS THE SPOT 159
PERFECT 170
COMPLETE LIST OF NO-HIT GAMES 183
INDEX 189

INTRODUCTION

*A no-hitter isn't merely a tremendous baseball feat. It is
a miracle. Out on the mound stands one man pitted
against matter, mind, the physical, yes, at times, it would
seem to be the occult, too.*

*Up at the plate come big men, strong men, cunning
ones, predominantly physical men and intellectual ones,
as well. They swing some two pounds of solid wood at
pitch after pitch, they hit the ball more or less regularly,
though they miss it utterly on many occasions. That
little ball is caught in the outfield and thrown for outs in
the infield. Yet, never a hit.*

*Yes, it's miraculous and I'll never stop wondering
at it.*

— Dan Daniel, Dean of American Baseball Writers

It is autumn in New York. The sun is shining, but
there is a chill in the air, an unmistakable sign that
winter is not far off.

Up in the Bronx, in old and stately Yankee
Stadium, where great American folk heroes such as Babe
Ruth, Lou Gehrig, Joe DiMaggio, Lefty Gomez, and

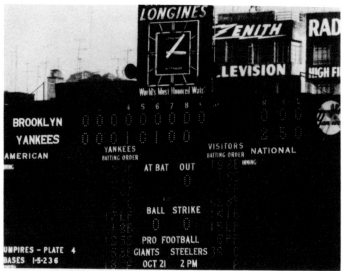

Yankee Stadium scoreboard tells the story. Don Larsen has just pitched the only perfect game in World Series history.

Red Ruffing once roamed, the crowd is buzzing with the excitement and anticipation of a World Series game.

But this is not just any World Series game. It is game number five of the 1956 World Series between the New York Yankees and their arch rivals from across the East River, the Brooklyn Dodgers.

The date is October 8, 1956. There are 64,519 fans in the huge ball park, their eyes focused on a tall young man standing on the pitcher's mound. He is Don Larsen and he is protecting a 2–0 lead, but that is not the full story, which is behind him on the giant scoreboard that reaches up to the sky and towers over the field.

The story is in the column for hits, and the number in that column on the Brooklyn Dodger line is a big, fat zero that stands out like the North Star on a clear, black night.

Through eight and two-thirds innings, Don Larsen has held the fearsome, slugging Dodgers without a hit. Not only have the Dodgers been hitless, but they have not even had a base runner. They have sent twenty-six batters up to hit, and Larsen has retired all twenty-six.

Now he prepares to pitch to Dale Mitchell, pinch-hitting for pitcher Sal Maglie, with the count no balls and two strikes. Larsen reaches back and pumps a fast ball toward the plate and Mitchell starts to swing, but checks. The right arm of home plate umpire Babe Pinelli shoots into the air and there is bedlam, as if the umpire's simple and familiar act has triggered an explosion.

The crowd bursts into a frenzied roar. Catcher Yogi Berra leaps into the air, then dashes for the pitcher's mound and throws his stubby body onto Larsen, who is soon swallowed up in a sea of arms and legs and bodies.

Don Larsen has pitched a perfect game. In one day . . . one game . . . two hours and six minutes of playing time, he has reached baseball's summit.

In 307 World Series games no pitcher had ever pitched a no-hitter. A perfect game was only a dream in the pressure of a World Series game. There had not been a perfect game even in the regular season since April 30, 1922, seven years before Larsen was born.

If a no-hitter is the triple crown of horse racing, the grand slam in golf, the hat trick in hockey, and the four-minute mile in track, a perfect game is all of these and more. It is Babe Ruth pointing to the right-field stands in the 1932 World Series and hitting the next pitch in the area where he had just pointed; it is Bobby Thomson's home run in the third game of the 1951 National League pennant play-off; it is Christy Mathewson pitching three World Series shutouts; it is Roger

Maris' sixty-first home run and Maury Wills' 104th stolen base. It is a once in a lifetime thing. There are no reruns.

A no-hitter is perfection. "It is," says Sandy Koufax, the only man in baseball history to pitch four of them, "a dream. It is the ultimate ambition of every pitcher."

In its way, a no-hitter is more difficult than hitting sixty home runs or stealing ninety-six bases or winning thirty games in a single season.

"I used to think I would get a bigger thrill out of striking out eighteen men in one game than pitching a no-hitter," Koufax said recently. "Then I struck out eighteen men and, believe me, the no-hitter is more thrilling. With the eighteen strikeouts, as with sixty home runs and ninety-six steals, if you miss one man or one day, you always have the next batter, the next day. The only thing comparable to a no-hitter is Joe Di-Maggio's fifty-six game hitting streak. If you miss, you must start over from scratch."

There is something mysterious about a no-hitter. It is a drama in nine acts that moves slowly toward a suspenseful climax. The drama continues to build because one mistake, one slip can end it all.

A no-hitter is one of the rarest feats in all of sports. A perfect game is probably the rarest. The odds against a pitcher pitching a no-hitter are overwhelming. The odds against a perfect game are astronomical.

Since the beginning of the modern era in baseball in 1901 through the 1967 season, there have been more than 85,000 games played in the major leagues. In that time there have been 129 no-hitters pitched, or approximately one no-hitter for every 660 games. The odds against a no-hitter, therefore, are about 1,320 to 1, since in every game there are two pitchers with a chance to pitch a no-hitter.

Similarly, in that time there have been six perfect games pitched in the major leagues (exclusive of the World Series), or one perfect game for every 14,166 games, making the odds against a perfect game about 28,000 to 1.

It is the dream of every pitcher to pitch a no-hitter, and the dream of every fan to witness one. Once you have seen a no-hitter, you never forget it.

There is no formula for pitching a no-hitter, just as there is no pattern for the men who have pitched them. You can get one with a good fast ball or a good curve ball or with hardly anything at all. There have been pitchers who thought from the first pitch they were going to get one and there have been pitchers who had nothing while warming up, then somehow found it during the game.

There is no restriction on who can or cannot pitch a no-hitter. Everybody starts from scratch, no previous experience required. Ernie Koob pitched one and he won only twenty-four big league games. But Grover Cleveland Alexander never pitched a no-hitter and he won 373 big league games. Lefty Grove, a 300-game winner, did not pitch one, but Bill McCahan, who won sixteen games, did.

Dizzy Dean won thirty games in one season and never pitched a no-hitter. Neither did Robin Roberts, who started more than six hundred games in the majors. But Bobo Holloman got one in his first major-league start and won only two other games in his career. Eddie Plank, Early Wynn, and Whitey Ford did not pitch a no-hitter; Cliff Chambers, Ed Head, and Bob Keegan did.

It is not necessary to be good to pitch a no-hitter. Given a choice between being either good or lucky, the latter is more likely to get you one.

"You need luck to pitch a no-hitter," says Sandy Koufax, who was more good than lucky. "The batters must hit the ball in the right direction, and you need the fielders behind you to make the plays."

It is rare that a no-hitter is achieved without some fielder making a sensational play, and there have been one-hitters, two-hitters, and three-hitters when not one ball was hit hard.

Luck? Yes, but that's what makes a no-hitter so thrilling. There are Hall of Famers who never pitched a no-hitter; but not every pitcher who has a no-hitter is in the Hall of Fame, although his feat is commemorated in baseball's shrine in Cooperstown, New York.

While a no-hitter gives a man a measure of immortality, it does not guarantee him permanent employment. In the nine years from 1958 through 1966, there were twenty-three no-hitters pitched by seventeen different pitchers, and thirteen of them were traded and told to be immortals somewhere else.

Three years after he pitched his perfect game in the World Series, Don Larsen was pitching for the Kansas City Athletics. The mighty had fallen; but for that one day, at least, he was the greatest pitcher in the history of baseball.

Records are made to be broken, but no-hitters live forever. Once a pitcher has pitched one, nobody can ever take it away from him. The happiest words that can be said of a pitcher are these: He once pitched a no-hitter.

ONE

SANDY

As a boy growing up in Bensonhurst, a middle-class section near Coney Island in Brooklyn, New York, Sanford Koufax mixed with all the other boys his age. When school was out in the summer, the boys in his neighborhood could be found on a nearby sandlot playing baseball, and Sandy Koufax was always among them. In the winter, after school, the boys in his neighborhood could be found in the Jewish Community House playing basketball and, again, Sandy Koufax was always among them.

Sandy's mother never worried about him. She always knew that he was out playing ball and that he would be home in time for dinner . . . or a little later.

Sandy was like most boys his age. He loved sports — all sports — and he dreamed of someday being a professional athlete.

In his mind he could hear the crowd cheering for him as he performed great feats of athletic skill. Usually he pictured himself in Madison Square Garden, playing professional basketball for the New York Knickerbockers, the arena jammed to the rafters, the fans roaring their approval as he drove in for a lay-up, and the public address announcer droning, "New York basket by Koufax."

Although he played all sports, basketball was Sandy's great love. By the time he entered Lafayette High School, he had grown almost to his full height of six feet, two inches, and he made the varsity basketball team.

By his senior year, he was the star of the team. One night, the New York Knickerbockers came to Bensonhurst to play a benefit scrimmage with the Lafayette team and Koufax was matched up with Harry Gallatin, the six-foot, six-inch muscleman of the Knickerbockers. Koufax played so well that Gallatin came to him after the game, took his name on a piece of paper, and announced to the happy and proud youngster, "I'm going to be looking for you in future years."

His friends were not surprised when he entered the University of Cincinnati in the fall of 1953 on a basketball scholarship. The real surprise was to come fourteen months later.

On December 14, 1954, the Brooklyn Dodgers announced they had signed Sanford Koufax, a left-handed pitcher from the University of Cincinnati by way of Brooklyn, to a bonus contract calling for a $14,000 bonus and a $6,000 salary for the first year. Not only were his friends, neighbors, and relatives confused. Sandy's head was swimming with the sudden turn of events.

Baseball had always been secondary in his life, something to keep him active after the basketball season. He had made the Lafayette varsity baseball team as a left-handed throwing, right-handed hitting first baseman. While his fielding was good and his height made him an excellent target at first base, Koufax was a terrible hitter.

On weekends, he played with a neighborhood team called the Tomahawks in the Ice Cream League, organized and run as a labor of love by a man named Pop Secol. The Tomahawks had one outstanding pitcher who pitched most of the games and his name was *not* Sandy Koufax.

One Saturday, the Tomahawks needed a pitcher for the second game of a double-header, and they drafted Koufax because he had a strong arm and could throw the ball harder than any other player on the team. For the first time, Sandy Koufax put his foot on a pitcher's mound, but he could hardly have been described as a promising pitcher. He was extremely wild. He walked eight batters in the first two innings. Sandy Koufax' debut was a 4–1 defeat.

That seemed to be the beginning and the end of Sandy's pitching career. He returned to his customary position, first base, at Lafayette and, the following season, with the Tomahawks. Two other times he was pressed into emergency duty as a pitcher for the Tomahawks, losing one game, 6–2, and finally winning one on

17

his third try, 4–2.

Nobody — Sandy included — thought of Koufax as a pitcher. Then along came Milt Laurie. Laurie had been a semipro player in Brooklyn during the 1930's. An automobile accident ended his career but could not diminish his love for the game. He devoted most of his free time to running a sandlot team which played in the Coney Island League. Laurie's two sons were high school teammates of Koufax' and their dad was a regular spectator at the school's games. Watching infield practice one day, Laurie was impressed with the strength of Koufax' throwing arm and invited him to play with his team, the Parkviews.

"You've got a big league arm," he told Sandy. "I'd like to work with you as a pitcher."

Sandy agreed to give it a try. In his three games as a pitcher for the Tomahawks he had come to like the position. A pitcher is the central man in the game. Unlike first base, pitching means continuous action. The pitcher is involved in every pitch; he is the switch that sets the wheels in motion. It makes a guy feel important.

The first time Koufax pitched for the Parkviews, he threw a no-hitter, which must be considered a preview of things to come. He could throw hard, there was no mistaking that. He was difficult to hit and he overmatched most of the batters he faced. He soon became the Parkviews' best pitcher, but he was his own worst enemy. Whenever he failed, it was because he lacked control.

While pitching for the Parkviews, Sandy was spotted by Jimmy Murphy, veteran Brooklyn sports columnist, who devoted a lifetime to writing about high school and sandlot sports in Brooklyn. An old semipro pitcher himself, Murphy was a good judge of pitching talent and he reported his discovery to Al Campanis, a scout for the Brooklyn Dodgers.

Campanis promised to follow up Murphy's tip, but soon a half dozen major league teams began to get word about the unknown Koufax boy who was practically unhittable in the Coney Island League.

That fall Sandy went on to the University of Cincinnati to become the third leading scorer on the freshman basketball team. After the season, he went out for baseball almost out of habit and made the team as a pitcher. In one game he set a school record by striking out eighteen batters. When school ended, he returned to Brooklyn to pitch for the Parkviews. By now the scouts were trailing him with more than casual interest.

The Pirates, Phillies, Yankees, Giants, and Braves all expressed a desire to sign him, but the Dodgers and Campanis got there first and with the most money. So, in the spring of 1955, Sandy Koufax reported to spring training at Vero Beach, Florida. He was nineteen years old and a Dodger although he had pitched no more than twenty games in his life.

Koufax was eager to get to Vero Beach. He was anxious to begin his professional baseball career, anxious to show what he could do. Spring training promised to be full of adventure. It turned out to be full of frustrations.

He discovered spring training was not all fun and games. It consisted of hard work, tedious exercises, and cramming knowledge into his head.

Sandy's problems that first spring were no different from the problems any young pitcher might face. He threw hard, but he was wild and he had so much to

19

learn. In Koufax' case the problems were exaggerated, partly because he had so little experience as a pitcher and partly because he found himself in a touchy situation that was not of his own making.

After the war, the country's economy boomed and baseball enjoyed the prosperity that went along with it. Business was at its high point, and many ball clubs began shelling out staggering sums of money to untried bonus babies. The successful clubs kept pouring their profits into new talent, cornering the market on the best youngsters and flooding their farm systems with them. This kept an unending supply of talent streaming to the team that could afford the tariff, but the poor teams remained poor.

Baseball decided to do something about the situation, and, in the process, almost dried up the minor leagues, the lifeblood of baseball. Organized baseball ruled that any team giving a player more than $4,000 as a bonus would have to carry that player on its roster for two full seasons. The purpose was to prevent the wealthy clubs from cornering the market on all the talent. This rule penalized the young player. Those who got the big bonuses were deprived, for two years, of the opportunity to learn their trade in the minor leagues. The others, who might have been given a sizable bonus, were held below $4,000.

The rule required that, for 1955 and 1956, Sandy Koufax should be a major-league ballplayer. That is, he would get the minimum major-league salary, wear the uniform of a major-league team, sit in the dugout, travel

He was at the University of Cincinnati on a basketball scholarship, but one spring day Sandy Koufax struck out 18 men.

with and appear on the roster of a major-league team. Even Sandy, himself, would admit he was far from being a major leaguer in 1955. All he was doing was occupying space that could have been used to greater advantage by a veteran player.

The Dodgers had been at or near the top of the National League every year since World War II ended. Usually they were in a race that went right down to the final day of the season.

They won the 1949 pennant on the final day, lost the 1950 pennant on the final day, and lost the 1951 pennant in a play-off with their arch rivals, the New York Giants. The Dodgers won in 1952 and 1953, but the hated Giants beat them out in 1954. As the 1955 season began, the Dodgers were determined to reclaim the National League title.

It was predominantly a veteran Dodger team, sparked by the fire of Jackie Robinson; the leadership of PeeWee Reese; the power of Roy Campanella, Gil Hodges, Duke Snider, and Carl Furillo; and the pitching of Don Newcombe and Carl Erskine. It was no place for a nineteen-year-old rookie.

In the first few weeks, Koufax enjoyed his stay in the big leagues. For sixty-five games, all he had to do was sit around and watch the Dodgers destroy the rest of the league. By their sixty-sixth game, on June 24, 1955, the Dodgers were leading the league by fourteen games when the name Sandy Koufax appeared in a major-league box score for the first time.

In the last of the fifth inning in Milwaukee, the Dodgers trailed the Braves, 7–1, when Koufax walked into the game. He quickly filled the bases, then proceeded to mow down the next six Braves in order. In his next outing, he again loaded the bases with nobody out and escaped without allowing a run. Sandy was beginning to get the idea that pitching in the major leagues was no different than pitching in the Coney Island League.

But he soon discovered the difference. When he was awarded a starting assignment against the Pittsburgh Pirates, his control got him in trouble and Sandy was knocked out by the sixth inning.

He was returned to the bullpen for a few stints and earned another chance to start, this time against the Cincinnati Reds. Sandy struck out fourteen Reds and held them to two hits. It was to be the young left-hander's only memorable experience of the year. His entire contribution to the Dodgers' 1955 pennant drive was 12 games, 42 innings, two victories, two defeats, 30 strikeouts, and 28 walks.

The 1956 season was not much better. Sandy was in 16 games, pitched 59 innings, won two, lost four, struck out 30 and walked 29.

If nothing else, Sandy was learning his way around the National League, but he hardly terrorized enemy batters. Still, the Dodgers kept him around for the 1957 season in which Sandy worked in 34 games, won five, lost four, struck out 122, and walked 51.

In 1958, the Dodgers left Brooklyn, moving west to Los Angeles. Koufax, the Brooklyn boy, looked forward to the switch. He hoped a change of scenery would do his pitching some good. Sandy was starting his fourth season; as old Dodger heroes vanished, opportunity increased and Koufax got more chances to pitch. He showed tantalizing flashes of brilliance. On August 31, 1959, he set a National League record and tied Bob

Feller's major-league mark by striking out eighteen Giants. And in the fifth game of the 1959 World Series, he pitched brilliantly against the Chicago White Sox, losing 1–0, with the winning run coming across on a double play.

But there were more bad days than good ones, and when the 1960 season ended Koufax showed a record of thirty-six victories and forty defeats for six big league seasons. Unable to crack the starting rotation, he was unhappy and frustrated. He thought about quitting and he even asked to be traded. But he was only twenty-five, his arm was sound, and he could throw as hard as anyone in baseball, so the Dodgers refused to give up on him.

The turning point came in the spring of 1961. Koufax was scheduled to pitch a B squad game against the Minnesota Twins. On the short trip to the Twins' training base, Sandy found himself sitting next to his friend, catcher Norm Sherry.

"I've been thinking of something," Sherry said. "This is just a B game today. You have nothing to lose. If you get behind the hitters, don't try to throw hard because when you do, your fast ball comes in high. Just once try it my way. If you get in trouble, let up and throw the curve ball to spots instead of trying to fire the ball past the hitter."

Sandy had heard this all before; but this time it sank in and he tried it Sherry's way. The results were exciting. He seemed to be throwing easily, but the ball went just as hard. He set the Twins down without a hit for seven innings. It did wonders for his confidence.

Whether it was Sherry's advice or maturity or the natural development after six years of struggle and hard work, nobody knows for sure. But Sandy Koufax became a pitcher in 1961. He might have made it without Sherry's advice, but you could not convince Sandy of that.

In 1961, he won eighteen games and lost thirteen and set a National League record by striking out 269 batters in 256 innings. After six hard, frustrating years, Sandy Koufax was suddenly a star, looked upon as one of the bright young pitchers in the National League. Experts nodded knowingly, insisting they had known all the time that, one day, Sandy would make it big.

Koufax eagerly awaited the start of spring training in 1962. Dodger manager Walt Alston had told the press during the winter that Sandy was not only to be in the starting rotation, he was being counted on to help bring the Dodgers another pennant.

On April 24, he became the first pitcher in baseball history to strike out eighteen batters in a game on two occasions as he shot down the Chicago Cubs at Wrigley Field.

Then came the night of June 30, 1962. Koufax went out to pitch against the New York Mets in Los Angeles' Dodger Stadium. In the first inning, Sandy threw nine pitches and struck out Richie Ashburn, Rod Kanehl, and Felix Mantilla. Inning after inning, the Mets went down futilely, helpless against Sandy's overpowering fast ball, his baffling curve, his tantalizing change of pace. As he went through the middle innings, Sandy still had not allowed a hit and the crowd's roar grew in intensity with each out.

In the seventh, he abandoned the curve ball and change-up and threw nothing but fast balls. Sandy was getting close to a no-hitter and he wanted it badly.

"I'd have shot myself if somebody got a hit off a

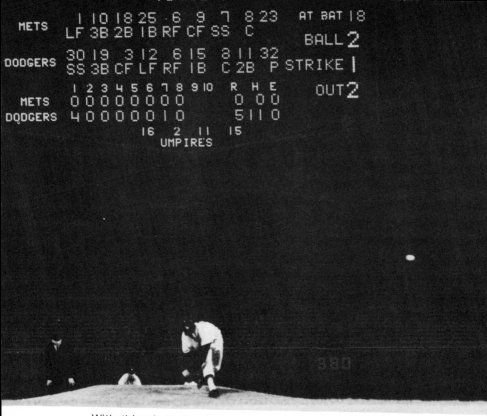

| METS | 1 10 18 25 6 9 7 8 23 | AT BAT 18 |
| | LF 3B 2B 1B RF CF SS C | BALL 2 |

DODGERS 30 19 3 12 6 15 8 11 32
SS 3B CF LF RF 1B C 2B P STRIKE 1

	1 2 3 4 5 6 7 8 9 10	R H E	OUT 2
METS	0 0 0 0 0 0 0	0 0 0	
DODGERS	4 0 0 0 0 1 0	5 1 0	

16 2 11 15
UMPIRES

With this pitch, Sandy achieved a no-hitter against the Mets, the first of a record four thrown in consecutive seasons.

change-up," he admitted.

He went into the ninth and retired Ashburn for the first out. Only Rod Kanehl and Felix Mantilla stood between him and no-hit glory. He bore down on Kanehl, who was one of those pesky slap hitters, the kind who always got a piece of the ball and could punch it over the infielders' heads or past them on the ground.

Kanehl did not hit the fast ball solidly and grounded out to shortstop. Now Mantilla. Koufax remembered the time that spring when Mantilla beat him with a line drive single to left.

"Keep him from pulling the ball," Sandy said to

26

himself. He fired a fast ball. "Oh, oh," he thought, "I got that one too close. . . ." But Mantilla hit over the ball and it was on the ground to third . . . the throw to first . . . and the game was over. Less than two years before, Sandy Koufax had thought of quitting. Now he sat on top of the baseball world with his first no-hitter!

"Either he throws the fastest ball I've ever seen," said Richie Ashburn, "or I'm going blind."

There was nothing wrong with Ashburn's eyesight.

By mid-season Koufax had won fourteen games. He was a cinch to win twenty and set a record for strikeouts, but then bad luck struck. Sandy began to notice a numbness on the tip of his left index finger. Then the finger began to blister and peel. He could not hold the ball properly. Something had blocked off the flow of blood to his left hand, and, for a time, it was feared Sandy might lose the finger. Doctors operated to save the finger, but Koufax was through pitching for the season — maybe forever.

Without him, the Dodgers lost the pennant to the Giants in a play-off, but they were more concerned with the future of their star left-hander. To have worked so hard and waited so long for success, then to have this happen seemed more than unfair.

Doctors managed to restore the flow of blood and told Koufax he would pitch again, but there was a wave of doubt that Sandy would ever be the pitcher he had been in the first half of the 1962 season. Only time would tell, and Sandy wasted little of it erasing those doubts.

On the second day of the 1963 season he beat the Cubs, 2–1, on a five-hitter. Two starts later, he beat the Cubs again, shutting them out and striking out fourteen.

Veins taut in
his neck, Koufax is
the picture of deter-
mination as he prepares
to throw one of his
explosive pitches.

Sandy rarely threw
sidearm, and his straight
overhand delivery made
his downbreaking curve
ball especially
effective.

His sixth start of 1963 came against the Giants in Los Angeles on May 11. Koufax never considered this one of his great games. He struck out only four men, surprisingly few for him, and walked one batter. But when the game ended, he had not allowed a hit. It was his second no-hitter in two years.

This was a year to remember. Koufax won twenty-five and lost only five. He broke his own strikeout record with 306 and walked only 58 in 311 innings. He led the National League with an earned run average of 1.88, was named the Most Valuable National League Player and the Cy Young Memorial Award winner as the outstanding pitcher in baseball. In the first game of the World Series, he struck out fifteen Yankees to set a World Series record and he pitched the fourth game to clinch the Series for the Dodgers in four straight.

Sandy Koufax was the biggest name in sports that winter. He was honored at banquets all over the country. Few ballplayers had ever captured the imagination of the public as had the handsome, Brooklyn-born bachelor, a modest hero and a deserving one. He had waited a long time for his big moment. He had prepared for it with hard work and had suffered great disappointments, but he wore his success well. His name was worth an increase in attendance of at least 10,000 fans each time he pitched.

But he was unable to remain free of injury. In 1964, he hurt his shoulder early in the season. He recovered and the doctors pronounced him fit, but again there was serious doubt that he was the Sandy Koufax of old, particularly since he had a 5–4 record as he waited to pitch against the Phillies in Philadelphia on the night of June 4.

He was perplexed by his record. The shoulder felt fine and he was unable to figure out what the trouble was.

Sitting in the Philadelphia clubhouse waiting to go out to warm up, Koufax began flipping through some old baseball magazines. In one, he noticed a sequence of pictures of his delivery in the no-hitter against the Giants. Suddenly it hit him.

He studied the pictures and realized he had not been opening up when he delivered — he was planting his right foot too far to the left when he followed through, throwing across his body. He went out to pitch, concentrating on placing his right foot several inches to the right.

He had found the secret! He allowed one man to reach base — Richie Allen, who walked but was immediately thrown out attempting to steal. Koufax pitched to the minimum twenty-seven batters and chalked up his third no-hitter. In all the years of baseball, only Larry Corcoran, Cy Young, and Bob Feller had pitched three no-hitters.

Koufax was now established as one of the truly great pitchers in baseball history, but he still could not rid himself of the injury jinx. On August 8, he slid into second base and landed hard on his left elbow. He dismissed the injury and continued to pitch. A few weeks later, the pain was so severe he finally went to see the Dodgers' team physician. Sandy had won fifteen of his last sixteen decisions. He had no way of knowing that the slide had begun the arthritic condition in the elbow that would cut short his brilliant career.

Dr. Robert Kerlan advised Koufax to forget pitching for the remainder of the 1964 season and to continue treatment with the hope that rest and medication would make the arm strong for 1965. Sandy agreed, since the Dodgers were buried deep in the second division with no hope of getting out.

There was the customary apprehension as Sandy waited for spring training, 1965. For the first three weeks, he could pitch without pain, but constant work made the elbow flare up. It was swollen after every pitching session. Dr. Kerlan decided that the only way to avoid the swelling was to give Sandy a shot in the elbow before he pitched. Then, after he had finished pitching, he was to put on a rubber sleeve and dunk the arm in a tub of ice water.

On the fourth day of the season he made his first start, beating the Phillies, 6–2. There were no after-effects. By August 10, Sandy had won twenty games and lost only four.

"Some sore elbow," said Cincinnati manager, Dick Sisler. "It's sore except between the first and ninth innings."

Little did Sisler know that in jest, he was speaking the truth. Dr. Kerlan was able to arrest the arthritis long enough for Koufax to pitch. With shots and medication, the elbow could be fixed so that Sandy could pitch every four days without pain and without swelling. On the other three days, there was agony.

Sandy punished himself, endangering his health, because the Dodgers were involved in one of their typi-cal cliff-hanging pennant races, bunched with the Giants, Pirates, Reds, and Braves.

As they prepared to meet the Chicago Cubs on the night of September 9, the Dodgers were tied for second place with the Reds, one-half game behind the Giants.

Each victory was precious, each defeat painful. Sandy Koufax was to be the pitcher. He had lost his last three starts, and the Dodgers were hoping desperately that their ace would snap out of his slump and put them back on the winning path.

He was up against Bob Hendley, another hard-throwing left-hander. For four innings, neither side had a hit. In the fifth, the Dodgers scored a run without getting a hit. They did not get a hit until Lou Johnson blooped a double in the seventh. Meanwhile, Koufax had retired all twenty-one Cubs he faced.

There were 29,139 fans in Dodger Stadium that night and they buzzed excitedly as Koufax went out to face the Cubs in the eighth. It was a big game in the pennant race, but to the fans it was more than that.

Koufax faced hard-hitting Ron Santo, who was called out on strikes for the twenty-second consecutive out. Ernie Banks struck out and so did Byron Browne. Three more men to get.

In the ninth, Koufax faced catcher Chris Krug and struck him out. Sandy seemed to be getting stronger. He threw three pitches to pinch-hitter Joey Amalfitano, who missed them all. Now it was the veteran Harvey Kuenn, pinch-hitting for the pitcher, the last man for Koufax to get for a perfect game. Again he made three pitches — all strikes. Sandy Koufax had pitched his fourth no-hitter and he had made it a perfect game, finishing the job by striking out the last six men.

"When Sandy's right," said his pitching partner Don Drysdale, "I'm surprised when he doesn't strike everybody out. It wouldn't surprise me if he pitched a no-hitter every time he went out there."

The game seemed to give the Dodgers the impetus

they needed. They went on to win the pennant on the next to last day of the season, Koufax pitching his twenty-sixth victory to clinch it. In the World Series, he lost the second game, but won the fifth and the seventh games against the slugging Minnesota Twins, twice pitching shutouts with only two days' rest.

It was a remarkable year. Sandy Koufax, a victim of arthritis, had pitched with courage and determination to take his place, once again, at the top of the baseball world.

It was a sad day when Sandy announced his retirement, but at one point he managed a wan smile.

By the middle of the 1966 season, it was clear to Sandy that he was playing his last season. It was not obvious to anyone else, however, because Sandy won twenty-seven games, including the pennant clincher on the final day of the season against the Philadelphia Phillies. But the pain and swelling had become more severe and the shots and medication more frequent. He made his decision with six weeks left in the season.

"It's not getting any better and there is no cure for it," he confided to friends. "I don't want to spend the rest of my life a cripple."

On November 18, 1966, six weeks before his thirty-first birthday and at an age when he should have had his best years before him, Sandy Koufax — to the regret of the entire baseball world — announced his retirement from baseball.

In twelve seasons, he had won 165 games and lost 87 and he had struck out 2,396 batters. The statistics do not tell the full story of the greatness of this pitcher. Nor do they tell of the heartbreak and frustration of the early years and the pain and suffering of the last years.

The true measure of Sandy Koufax as a pitcher is his record of four no-hitters, more than any other pitcher in baseball history.

TWO

GEORGE WASHINGTON PITCHED HERE

The excited fans filing out of the St. Louis ball park on that July 15, 1876, could not hide their astonishment or control their ecstasy. They had just seen something incredible. George Washington Bradley had completed nine full innings of pitching against the Hartford club and had not allowed a single safe hit.

The National League was not yet three months old, but the happy St. Louis rooters knew they had been witnesses to something extraordinary, something miraculous.

Word spread rapidly to the other cities in the embryonic baseball league and for days in Philadelphia, Boston, Louisville, New York, Cincinnati, Hartford, and Chicago, everyone talked about the wondrous St. Louis happening. When the first season ended without another pitcher matching the accomplishment, it was agreed that Bradley's game had been a freak, something that was not likely to happen ever again in the history of baseball.

George Washington Bradley is generally regarded as the father of the no-hitter, but somewhere there must be a place for Joseph Borden.

Poor Joe Borden. History dealt him a cruel blow, for it was Joseph Emley Borden, also known as Joseph Emley Josephs, who pitched the first recorded no-hitter on July 28, 1875, when he defeated Chicago for Philadelphia, 4–0. But that was in the old National Association during the dark ages of the sport. Bradley's no-hitter stands as the first because it was achieved in the National League's inaugural season.

However, Hall of Fame historian Lee Allen uncovered some facts to prove that Borden beat Bradley to the no-hitter by two months in 1876, but the game was not recognized; and to this day, despite Allen's evidence, it does not appear on any complete list of no-hitters.

According to Allen, Borden pitched the National League's first no-hitter for Boston on May 23, 1876, in an 8–0 victory over Cincinnati. The reason it was not recognized is that the box score shows two hits in the game for Cincinnati. Allen explains the mix-up in his book, *100 Years of Baseball.*

"Although the game was played at Boston," Allen writes, "the score was sent to the league office by Oliver

Perry Caylor, a writer for *The Cincinnati Enquirer*, and during the season Caylor, at variance with contemporary scorers, counted bases on balls as hits. Later, in 1887, bases on balls were to count as hits, but in the league's first campaign only Caylor scored them as such. Borden granted passes to two Cincinnati batters, passes which appeared as hits in the box score."

The box score in question shows another characteristic of the times: Twenty errors were made in the game, but nine of them were charged to catchers because passed balls in 1876 were charged as errors. Two other errors were charged to Borden because wild pitches were also charged as errors.

After his two "no-hitters," poor Joe Borden fell on the kind of bad times that typified his unhappy fate as a player, and he slipped into the shadowy past. He suffered a sore arm later that season and finished out the year as groundskeeper of the Boston ball park. A few years later, he turned up in a Philadelphia factory stitching baseballs like those he once threw past opposing batters. He died in 1889, a victim of the famous Johnstown flood.

For nearly four years after Bradley's 1876 no-hitter, no pitcher could duplicate the feat, strengthening the original belief that baseball would never see another such masterful performance.

Then, on June 12, 1880, John Lee Richmond, a graduate of Brown University pitching for Worcester, not only held Cleveland without a hit, but retired twenty-seven batters in a row without a runner reaching first base safely. It was baseball's first perfect game.

Just five days later another college man, John Montgomery Ward, a graduate of Penn State, duplicated the feat for Providence against Buffalo. Although there were to be five perfect games in the American League in the next eighty years, not until 1959 was the National League to see another perfect nine innings.

When Lawrence J. Corcoran of Chicago and James F. Galvin of Buffalo pitched no-hitters on consecutive days in August of 1880, the baseball lawmakers decided the pitcher had too much of an advantage over the hitter. They agreed to move the pitching rubber from forty-five feet to fifty feet from the plate. Apparently they achieved the desired result, because in 1881 no pitcher hurled a no-hitter.

But it did not take the pitchers long to catch up with the hitters and in 1882, with a second league — the American Association — now in operation, there were three no-hitters, including the second one by Corcoran, who proved the pitching distance made little difference to him.

Two years later, Corcoran, a native of Brooklyn, New York, became the first pitcher to throw three no-hitters. It was a record that would be tied twice, but not surpassed until eighty-one years later by another Brooklyn boy, Sandy Koufax.

Later in 1884, Edward Morris and Frank T. Mountain pitched no-hitters for Columbus in the American Association, the first time two different pitchers from the same team pitched no-hitters in the same year.

On October 4, 1891, a young left-hander named Ted Breitenstein made his first major-league start for St. Louis against Louisville and became the first pitcher to make his starting debut a hitless gem. A year later Charles (Bumpus) Jones of Cincinnati pitched a no-hitter in his first major-league appearance. Breitenstein pitched his second no-hitter in 1898 for Cincinnati and became the first southpaw pitcher of distinction.

With three no-hitters pitched in the 1891 and 1892 seasons, once again the baseball lords extended the pitching distance, this time to sixty feet, six inches, where it has remained to this day — although it has never been satisfactorily explained why they chose such an odd distance.

Again the move had the desired effect and there was just one no-hitter pitched in 1893 and none in the next three seasons.

Then, on September 18, 1897, a young man named Denton True Young pitched his first no-hitter for Cleveland against Cincinnati. By that time, Young had developed into quite a pitching sensation, having won 36 games in 1892, 32 in 1893, and 35 in 1895.

In 1890, Young, fresh off an Ohio farm, had gone to the manager of the Canton club in the Tri-State League and asked for a tryout. The manager consented, put on a glove, and asked Young to throw a few to him.

According to baseball legend, Young's first pitch whizzed by the manager's ear. A few more pitches zipped by so fast, the manager could not see them and they smashed into the wooden stands, breaking the boards.

When the club's owner came by, he noticed the damage and said, "What's been going on here? Looks like a cyclone's been through here."

"Sure has and there he is," replied the manager, pointing at Young. "You better sign that young cyclone right away."

"Hey, Cy," shouted the owner, "come over here."

Cy Young won 291 games in the National League; and in 1901, when baseball's modern era began with the formation of the American League, Cy jumped to the

new league and won 220 more games. He pitched until he was forty-four and won 511 big-league games, a record that, it is safe to say, will never be broken.

Earl L. Moore has the distinction of having pitched the first no-hitter in the modern era and the first in the American League for Cleveland against Chicago on May 9, 1901. However, it was a dubious distinction because after nine hitless innings, he lost the game in the tenth.

The first winning no-hitter under the present two-league setup was pitched by Christy Mathewson of the New York Giants, who blanked the St. Louis club, 5–0, on July 15, 1901, twenty-five years to the day after George Washington Bradley's first National League classic.

It was fitting that the first perfect game in modern times should be pitched by the incomparable Cy Young for Boston against Philadelphia on May 5, 1904. Four years later, Young became the second pitcher, and the first in modern times, to pitch three no-hitters.

The year 1914 saw the formation of a third league, the Federal League, and in its two years of existence there were five no-hitters. But many historians refuse to recognize them or list them because the league was notorious for sloppy play and scoring laxity.

In the six years from 1914–1919, there were twenty-four no-hitters (including five in the Federal League) with a peak of seven in 1917, the most ever pitched in any year during the modern era. In 1920, the lawmakers went to work again to legislate against the pitcher and banned the spitball, not only to take an advantage away

Nobody won more games than Cy Young, who pitched three no-hitters among his 511 victories.

from the pitcher, but for sanitary and safety reasons as well. In the six years following the spitball ban, there were only seven no-hitters pitched.

But once again, pitchers being an inventive and constantly improving lot, there were 13 no-hitters pitched in the 13 years from 1929 to 1941. Following World War II, pitchers broke out with a rash of no-hitters — 15 in the first seven postwar years.

On July 1, 1951, Bob Feller of the Cleveland Indians became the third pitcher in baseball history to pitch three no-hitters and the first to pitch all three in this century. He pitched his first one on the first day of the 1940 season and notched his second six years and one war later.

It is interesting to note that despite the advent of the lively ball, during a period when home runs flourished, the number of no-hitters increased rather than decreased.

In the eight-year period from 1960 to 1967 there were twenty-three no-hitters in both major leagues, four of them by Sandy Koufax of the Los Angeles Dodgers, a record for pitching excellence.

In fact, not since 1949 has a season passed without at least one no-hitter being pitched, an indication that there will be no end to what George Washington Bradley — or Joseph Emley Borden — started almost a century ago.

THREE

TWO OF A KIND

*Spahn...Bunning...Mathewson...Reynolds...
Trucks...Erskine...Maloney*

Pitching a no-hitter is a rare and distinguished accomplishment. Pitching two is a triumph of staggering proportions. Only fourteen pitchers have done it in the modern era. Here are the profiles on seven of the men who have pitched two no-hitters.

Better Late Than Never

At the age of forty, most ballplayers are sitting around the fireplace of a comfortable home, smoking a

This was during first of Warren Spahn's two no-hitters—against the Phils—when the Brave ace was 39 years old.

pipe and spinning stories of great moments in years gone by. Not Warren Spahn. At the age of forty he was still spinning his curve ball past National League hitters — many of them younger than his own son — on his way to winning more major-league games than any left-hander in the history of baseball.

On April 28, 1961, five days after his fortieth birthday, Warren Spahn of the Milwaukee Braves beat the Giants in San Francisco by the score of 1–0. It was his second no-hitter. He had pitched his first just seven months before — on September 16, 1960 — against the Philadelphia Phillies. By that time he had been the winning pitcher in almost three hundred big league games.

Warren Spahn did not get things done in a hurry, but he got them done.

44

Spahn did not win his first big-league game until he had passed his twenty-fifth birthday. In most cases, if a pitcher has not made it by that time, he is told, politely but firmly, to look for another line of work. But in Warren's case there was a good reason for the late start. It was called World War II.

He had signed with the Boston Braves right out of South Park High School in Buffalo, New York, at the age of nineteen. Almost immediately, Spahn showed tremendous promise. In his second year of professional ball he won nineteen games for Evansville and the following year he won seventeen games and lost twelve for Hartford, the Braves' top farm team. This record earned him a promotion to the varsity at the end of the 1942 season, where he worked sixteen innings and was looked over by the well-trained eye of the Braves' veteran manager, Casey Stengel.

"The boy," Stengel said sagely, "has a great future in this game."

But the future had to wait. Later that year, Spahn went into the army and marched off to war. He won a battlefield commission as second lieutenant and did not return to the baseball wars until the 1946 season had started.

Warren got a passing grade in his rookie year, winning eight and losing five without benefit of spring training. By 1947 he was a star, combining with veteran Johnny Sain to give the Braves the most feared one-two pitching combination in the National League. From 1947 to 1950, Spahn won seventy-eight games and Sain won seventy-five, and Braves' fans adopted a fight slogan which was to become legendary: "Spahn and Sain, then pray for rain."

After 1951, Sain was gone but Spahn carried on, now with a new pitching partner, Lou Burdette. Starting in 1956, Spahn won twenty or more games for six consecutive seasons and helped the Milwaukee Braves (the Braves moved from Boston to Milwaukee after the 1952 season) win National League pennants in 1957 and 1958. In the 1958 World Series, he pitched a two-hit shutout against the New York Yankees in the fourth game, and his mastery over the Bombers was so convincing it prompted veteran sports columnist Red Smith to comment in the sixth inning, "This is the only 1–0 rout in the history of baseball."

In his major-league career, Spahn won more games, pitched more shutouts, worked more innings, compiled more twenty-victory seasons, and struck out more batters than any southpaw in the history of baseball. But his greatest thrills came when he pitched his no-hitters in consecutive seasons. He had waited a long time to achieve the goal of all pitchers. To Warren Spahn, it was well worth the wait.

Father's Day

On Sunday, June 21, 1964, Mrs. Mary Bunning and her oldest daughter, Barbara, age twelve, drove seventy-five miles on the New Jersey Turnpike to New York's Shea Stadium to watch Barbara's dad pitch the first game of a double-header against the New York Mets. The six other Bunning children remained at home in the Bunning's apartment in Cherry Hill, New Jersey.

Barbara and her mother watched the Philadelphia Phillies score a run in the first inning and one in the second, while Jim Bunning retired the Mets in order.

With one out in the fifth, Bunning still had not allowed a base-runner and Met catcher Jesse Gonder sent a hard smash toward right field. But second baseman Tony Taylor made a dive for the ball, smothered it on the outfield grass, picked himself up, and threw Gonder out by two steps. This game was going to be something special. Jim Bunning sensed it. The 32,026 fans sensed it, and Mary Bunning sensed it.

It was so much like the other time — six years ago on July 20, 1958. There were only four Bunning children

Jim Bunning, who had no-hitters in both the American and National Leagues, was never bothered by an awkward follow-through.

Jim pitched his first no-hitter for Detroit in 1958 and his second for the Phillies six years later—a perfect game on Father's Day.

then and Jim was pitching for the Detroit Tigers against the Boston Red Sox at Fenway Park in Boston. It was also the first game of a Sunday double-header and he beat the Red Sox, 3–0, with a no-hitter. It was the first time the Sox had had a no-hitter thrown against them in their home park in thirty-two years.

Jim had spent nine years in Detroit, winning 118 games for the Tigers and twice leading the American League in strikeouts. After the 1963 season, in which he had slumped to twelve victories and thirteen defeats — after winning nineteen games in 1962 — he was traded to Philadelphia.

It had been like starting a new life, and the adjustment was difficult for Mrs. Bunning and the seven little Bunnings. It meant disrupting a routine Mrs. Bunning had followed since she and Jim were married. It meant finding a new apartment close to Philadelphia where she and the children could spend the summer until school opened and they had to return to their permanent home in Ft. Thomas, Kentucky. The Bunnings had been in New Jersey only a few days when the Phillies were scheduled to play in New York, and Mrs. Bunning decided it would be a good day to drive up for the game.

In the sixth inning, Jim retired the Mets in order again, and Mary Bunning twisted her handkerchief nervously.

In the Mets' seventh, Jim Hickman struck out. Ron Hunt grounded to third. Ed Kranepool struck out. In the eighth, Joe Christopher struck out. Jesse Gonder grounded to second. Bob Taylor struck out.

"I'd like to borrow Sandy Koufax' hummer (fast ball) for this last inning," Bunning said to catcher Gus Triandos as he went out for the ninth inning.

Charlie Smith led off and popped to shortstop Cookie Rojas. A tense crowd watched Bunning motion for Triandos to come to the mound.

"Tell me a joke," Bunning said. "Say something, just give me a breather."

George Altman pinch-hit for Amado Samuel and struck out.

Now there was just one out to go and Johnny Stephenson pinch-hit for Tom Sturdivant. The first pitch was a curve . . . strike one, swinging. The next pitch was taken for strike two. Bunning tried to hit the low, outside corner, but missed for ball one. Again, he missed the corner for ball two.

In the stands, Mary Bunning anxiously watched her husband turn his back to the plate to gaze at the scoreboard. He adjusted his cap. He was ready. Curve ball . . . Stephenson swung . . . Strike three!

In the stands, Mary Bunning burst into tears of joy. On the mound, Jim Bunning pounded his fist into his glove and dashed toward Triandos, hand outstretched to take the victory ball.

It was a perfect game, only the eighth in baseball history — the first in the National League in eighty-four years, the first in either league during the regular season in forty-two years. It belonged to Jim Bunning, father of seven, and it came, fittingly, on Father's Day.

Old Pitchers Never Die, They Fade Away

In every generation, one man stands out as the greatest pitcher of his time. But who is the greatest pitcher of all time?

Is it Cy Young, who won more games than any

other pitcher? Is it Sandy Koufax, who pitched more no-hitters than any other pitcher? Is it Walter Johnson, who struck out more batters than any other pitcher? Is it Warren Spahn, who won more games than any other left-hander? Or Grover Cleveland Alexander? Bob Feller? Lefty Grove?

There is much less debate about who was the game's greatest hitter. Almost unanimously, the choice is Babe Ruth. And the Babe, who conducted a one-man reign of terror on pitchers and whose opinion must therefore be carefully considered, once cast his vote for Christy Mathewson as baseball's greatest pitcher.

Connie Mack agreed with the Babe, and so did John McGraw — but his opinion could be prejudiced because it was the acquisition of Mathewson by McGraw that turned the New York Giants into the most successful team in baseball at the turn of the century.

John Kieran, sports writer for *The New York Times,* was not prejudiced, however, and he once wrote: "Matty was the greatest pitcher I ever saw. He was the greatest anybody ever saw. Let them name all the others. I don't care how good they were. Matty was better."

Mathewson, nicknamed "Big Six" after a famous New York City fire company, came to the Giants in 1901 after they had rejected him the year before. Matty learned to pitch as a boy on his family's farm in Factoryville, Pennsylvania. At the age of nine, he discovered he could make stones curve by twisting his wrist when he threw them.

He went on to star in football and baseball at Bucknell University and, upon graduation, signed to play professional baseball in Taunton, Massachusetts, in the summer of 1899. The following year he played at Nor-

When the New York Giants dominated the National League at the turn of the century, Christy Mathewson was their ace.

folk, Virginia, where he impressed the Giants, who purchased his contract for $1,500. But after six games he was returned to Norfolk.

Cincinnati gave him a chance in 1901, but was dissatisfied and put him up for trade. Given a second chance to obtain the young right-hander, the Giants took advantage of the opportunity, sending the aging veteran Amos Rusie to Cincinnati in return for Mathewson.

Employing his baffling fadeaway pitch, forerunner of the screwball, Matty won twenty and lost sixteen for the seventh-place Giants in 1901. On July 15 of that year

51

he pitched the first no-hitter in modern times, turning back St. Louis, 5–0.

Following a poor 1902 season, he won 20 or more games in the next twelve consecutive seasons. He won 30 or more games in three consecutive years from 1903 to 1905, and in 1908 he established the present National League record by winning 37 games.

On June 13, 1905, Matty became the first pitcher to hurl two no-hitters in the modern era when he beat the Chicago Cubs, 1–0.

Christy Mathewson brought a new stature and respect to the game of baseball, which had been looked upon as an outlaw sport played by irresponsible, shiftless vagabonds. He was a college man, a quiet, clean-living gentleman so devoutly religious that he refused to pitch on the Sabbath.

The renowned sports writer Grantland Rice once wrote: "Christy Mathewson brought something to baseball no one else had ever given the game — not even Babe Ruth or Ty Cobb. He handed the game a certain touch of class, an indefinable lift in culture, brains, personality. . . ."

Big for his day, at six feet, one and one-half inches, 195 pounds, intelligent, modest and extremely good-looking, Mathewson was the first of baseball's heroes.

In seventeen seasons he won 373 games, tying Grover Cleveland Alexander for the National League record. He struck out 2,505 batters and he pitched two no-hitters, but his shining hour came in baseball's first official World Series in 1905 against Connie Mack's Philadelphia Athletics.

Within the span of six days, Matty achieved something that has never been equalled. He pitched three consecutive shutouts, allowing fourteen hits, striking out eighteen, and walking one in twenty-seven innings.

"It was," wrote Grantland Rice, "the greatest single World Series pitching exhibition ever known."

Big Chief Strike-'Em-Out

Shadows fall quickly on Yankee Stadium in the autumn of the year, making high fly balls almost impossible to catch. Many a player's career has been tarnished by an inability to become accustomed to the lengthening shadows during day games in September and October.

On September 28, 1951, a typical autumn day, the New York Yankees took on the Boston Red Sox in Yankee Stadium. The huge ball park was splashed with bright sunshine as the game started. By the seventh inning, the entire infield and most of the outfield were darkened by shadows.

New York's ace pitcher, Allie (Wahoo) Reynolds, affectionately known as "The Chief" because he was part Creek Indian, pitched for the home side. As he pitched in the top of the ninth inning, he had not allowed a hit.

Earlier in the year, on July 12, Reynolds had pitched a no-hitter against the Cleveland Indians in a thrilling 1–0 duel with the great Bob Feller, just eleven days after Feller had pitched the third no-hitter of his illustrious career. Feller allowed the Yankees just four hits, one of them a seventh-inning home run by Gene Woodling, which was all Reynolds needed to win and put his no-hitter into the books.

Now, Allie had three outs to get against the Red Sox to become the first pitcher in thirteen years to pitch two no-hitters in the same season. Johnny Vander Meer had done so for the Cincinnati Reds in 1938.

It was the first game of a double-header and the Yankees held a commanding 8–0 lead, but there was much excitement in the stands. If the Yanks won both games, they would clinch their third straight American League pennant, but more exciting was the rare thrill of witnessing a no-hitter.

Reynolds disposed of the first two hitters in the explosive Red Sox batting order and prepared to face the fearsome Ted Williams, who batted .318 for the year. Allie quickly buzzed two strikes over with a blazing fast ball, the Chief's trademark.

Now the Super Chief was one strike away from his second no-hitter as he prepared to throw to Ted Wil-

Helping Allie Reynolds (in jacket) celebrate second no-hitter are Yank teammates Gene Woodling, Yogi Berra and Joe Collins.

liams. His fast ball was a blur, but Williams swung and got a piece of the ball, sending it twisting high behind home plate. Yogi Berra anxiously tore off his mask, threw it a safe distance away from the plate, and dashed back, looking up and trying to find the ball in the shadows.

The ball was twisting crazily as it fell at a rapid speed. Berra lunged with his glove and the ball hit the mitt, but he was off balance and the ball popped out of the mitt and plunked to the ground, giving Williams another chance to spoil the no-hitter.

"I wanted to crawl into a hole," Berra said later.

He went to the mound, but before Yogi could say a word, Reynolds patted him on the back and told him to forget it.

Reynolds pitched again . . . another fast ball . . . and again Williams sent a high, twisting foul behind home plate. Again Berra tossed his mask and planted his feet firmly, waiting for the ball to descend. He picked the ball out of the shadows as it hurtled down and plopped right in Yogi's mitt and he did not muff his second chance. He squeezed the ball, then leaped into the air and made a dash for the mound to embrace Allie Reynolds, who had pitched his second no-hitter in ten weeks.

The record books will not support Allie Reynolds as one of the game's great pitchers. He won 182 and lost 107 in a thirteen-year career and only once, in 1952, was he a twenty-game winner. But the Chief rates high as one of the game's all-time clutch pitchers.

He won seven and lost two in World Series competition, including a masterful 1–0, two-hit shutout over the Brooklyn Dodgers in the opening game of the 1949

Series. And he had his best years from 1949 to 1953, when the Yankees reeled off five consecutive world championships, winning eighty-three and losing only forty-one during that stretch.

Reynolds was considered a mediocre pitcher, winning fifty-one and losing forty-seven, when the Yankees got him from the Cleveland Indians in a surprise trade for second baseman Joe Gordon, following the 1946 season. Given a choice between Reynolds and Steve Gromek, the Yankees selected the Chief on the recommendation of Joe DiMaggio.

"He can buzz the high, hard one by me anytime he has a mind to," Joe D. said. "Reynolds is the one I'd take."

Yankee followers disapproved of the trade, since Gordon was one of the Stadium's all-time heroes and Reynolds was little more than a .500 pitcher. The Chief soon changed everyone's mind. He became a Yankee mainstay for eight years, while Gordon faded out of the major leagues after four more seasons.

Where's The Fire?

In the third inning, Phil Rizzuto swung and sent a slow roller to Detroit shortstop, Johnny Pesky, who charged the ball but had trouble getting it out of his glove. Rizzuto made it to first base safely.

"Error," said the official scorer, John Drebinger, the distinguished gentleman from *The New York Times*.

"Whaddya mean error?" challenged Dan Daniel of the *New York World Telegram*. "The ball got stuck in the webbing of his glove. You can't give a man an error for that. It has to be a hit."

Virgil Trucks makes with a pair of zeros after pitching his second no-hitter (against the Yankees) in same season, 1952.

For the next few minutes, the Yankee Stadium press box took on the sounds of a debate hall. Hit or error? Half the writers said "error," the other half agreed with Daniel. Daniel won out — as he usually did — and Drebinger changed his ruling to "hit."

Three more innings passed and the only "hit" Detroit pitcher Virgil Trucks had allowed was Rizzuto's disputed third-inning single. Others in the press box appealed to Drebinger to reconsider his decision. It would be a shame for a man to lose a no-hitter on a questionable play.

It was August 25, 1952, and it had been a terrible year for Virgil (Fire) Trucks. He was a thirty-three-year-old right-hander famous for his fast ball, but his arm now seemed to lack life. Trucks was struggling through the poorest season of his twelve-year career — although on May 15, against the Washington Senators, he had pitched nine hitless innings in a scoreless game. With two out in the last of the ninth, Vic Wertz hit the home run that made Trucks claim victory and his first no hitter.

Now he was pitching against the Yankees, only a debatable "hit" preventing him from trying to become the third man in baseball history to pitch two no-hitters in a single season.

Ironically, Virgil Trucks had pitched two no-hitters in one season in 1938. Then he was a nineteen-year-old fireballer playing for Andalusia in the Class D Alabama-Florida League.

Three years later, with Buffalo in the International League, he pitched nine and two-thirds innings of hitless ball against Montreal, then gave up a hit and a run in the tenth, losing the no-hitter and the ball game to Ed Head, who later pitched a major-league no-hitter for the Brooklyn Dodgers.

The debate continued in the press box at Yankee Stadium until someone suggested Drebinger call Pesky on the special telephone that connects the press box with the dugout.

"Let's hear what he has to say," it was suggested. "If he has an explanation, we'll consider it."

Drebinger called Pesky, who insisted he should have been charged with an error on the play. "I messed it up," Pesky said. "The ball didn't stick in my glove. I had it, but it squirted out of my hand."

On the strength of that admission, Drebinger reversed his decision from "hit" to "error," and Trucks went on to get his second no-hitter. He won only five games that season and lost nineteen, and the following year he was traded to the St. Louis Browns.

Virgil Trucks won 177 games in his big-league career. However 1952 was a season he was happy to forget except for two days, one in May and the other in August; and John Drebinger has never regretted the phone call he made and the decision he had to change.

"We're Witcha Oisk"

Once upon a time in a very strange land there was a baseball team called the Dodgers. The land was strange because it had almost three million inhabitants — yet it was not a city and its most important product was a baseball team.

The land was a borough in New York City called Brooklyn, a name synonymous with baseball in the long, long ago. Its teams were the kookiest, and its fans the most colorful in all of baseball.

One such fan was Phil Foster, a comedian, who helped spread the legend of the "Beloved Bums" by including them in his act. Foster's favorite player was pitcher Carl Erskine; and his favorite routine was playing the part of a typical Dodger fan sitting in the bleachers of the tiny, run-down, obsolete park called Ebbets Field, shouting encouragment to his favorite pitcher.

"Atta boy Oisk," he would shout in shrill Brooklynese. "We're witcha Oisk. We're witcha baby."

Carl Erskine was not the Brooklyn type. He was a small, quiet, scholarly-looking gentleman from Anderson, Indiana. Neither was he the Dodger type. He was a pitcher — the best they had — on a team that seemed to think a pitcher was there only because it was required by the rules.

From 1952 to 1956, the Dodgers were the scourge of the National League, dominating the game with speed and strength. There were Jackie Robinson and

PeeWee Reese, Duke Snider and Carl Furillo, Roy Campanella and Gil Hodges. And there was Oisk. He won seventy-six games during that stretch and helped the Dodgers win four pennants in five years.

On June 19, 1952, he pitched against the Chicago Cubs on a dark, overcast day. He set the Cubs down in order in the first two innings and as he started the third, it began to rain. He retired the first two batters, then faced opposing pitcher Willard Ramsdell. Hurrying to complete the necessary five innings for an official game, he walked Ramsdell on four pitches. Just then, the rain fell heavily, delaying the game for forty-four minutes.

When play resumed, Erskine returned to the mound and did not allow another Cub to reach base. He had pitched a no-hitter and only his haste had prevented it from being a perfect game.

Erskine's most memorable performance came in the third game of the 1953 World Series against the New York Yankees. He set a World Series record (later broken by Sandy Koufax) when he struck out fourteen

The Brooklyn Dodgers' Carl Erskine waits in dugout before going to the mound for final inning of his second no-hitter.

Yankee batters, including the great Mickey Mantle four times.

By 1956 injuries had begun to diminish Erskine's skills. He suffered from a chronic sore arm early in the year. On the morning of May 11, he awoke with a pain behind his right shoulder so severe he could not lift his arm to comb his hair.

On the following day he was scheduled to pitch against the New York Giants, the Dodgers' hated rivals. It was an assignment Erskine had looked forward to and he refused to ask to be excused. Instead, he took a shot of cortisone and went out to pitch, planning to go as far as he was able.

He got through the first inning with no trouble and pitched courageously through the next four innings without allowing a hit. Encouraged by his success, he pitched into the ninth and still had not allowed a hit. Miraculously, he needed three more outs to pitch his second no-hitter.

He retired the first two batters in the ninth and the only man between him and his second no-hit game was Alvin Dark, a dangerous hitter who seemed able to slap at the ball and hit it wherever he pleased. Erskine worked carefully and his third pitch to Dark was a sharp curve ball. The batter swung and smashed it right back to the mound. Erskine stabbed it, then ran halfway to first before throwing easily to Gil Hodges to complete his second no-hitter.

The 1956 season was the last good one for Carl Erskine. He won only nine more games after that and, in June of 1959, although only thirty-two years old and just twenty-eight days short of becoming a ten-year major leaguer, he announced his retirement.

Injuries had weakened his arm and made him totally ineffective. He could have hung on and continued to draw his salary for the remainder of the season, but Carl Erskine never asked for charity. His pride and his dedication to his team would not permit him to hang on as a sub-par pitcher.

"I regret this decision," he said, "but I am no longer able to help the team because I cannot give 100 per cent anymore."

And for Carl Erskine, anything less than 100 per cent was not enough.

If At First You Don't Succeed

It was the last half of the ninth inning of a scoreless tie on the afternoon of August 19, 1965, in Chicago's Wrigley Field. There were two outs, and the bases were full with Cubs as Cincinnati pitcher Jim Maloney pitched to Don Landrum with the winning run ninety feet from home.

The Cubs had not had a hit off Maloney in eight and two-thirds innings. The three runners on base had been put there by two walks and a hit batter, but the 11,342 partisan Cub fans were thinking less about witnessing a possible no-hitter than they were of seeing a Cub victory.

Maloney swung into his windup and fired his high, hard one and Landrum hit a lazy pop fly over the infield, which was taken by shortstop Leo Cardenas. Jim Maloney had pitched nine hitless innings, but there was not the usual joy that accompanies such a feat. As he walked off the mound the thought in his mind was, "Oh, no, not again."

The Mets' Johnny Lewis circles bases after hitting home run which ruined Reds' Jim Maloney's no-hitter in the eleventh.

Just two months before, on the night of June 14, in Cincinnati's Crosley Field, Jim had suffered the greatest heartbreak known to a pitcher. He had pitched ten innings of hitless, scoreless ball against the New York Mets, but the Reds had not scored either; in the eleventh, rookie outfielder Johnny Lewis broke Maloney's heart by hitting a home run over the center-field wall.

It went into the books as a ten-inning no-hitter for Jim Maloney, but he had lost the game — and there can be no joy if there is no victory. It had been a masterful performance. He struck out eighteen, tying a major-league record for strikeouts in an extra-inning game, and he was rewarded with a $1,000 raise on the spot.

But the disappointment was great for Maloney,

although he tried to shrug it off. "That's baseball, I guess," he said. "It's too bad we didn't win."

His teammates shared Jim's disappointment, blaming themselves for not being able to score a run for him. He had been the ace of the Cincinnati staff since coming up from San Diego in 1962 to win nine games. He could throw as hard as anyone in baseball, and in 1963 won twenty-three games and lost only seven. They admired and respected him for his courage and determination and for his conduct in the face of such a great disappointment. "Someday," they vowed, "we'll make it up to him."

That day came sixty-seven days later in Chicago. In the tenth inning, Cardenas hit a home run to give Maloney the run he needed, and he did not waste it. He retired the Cubs without a hit in the tenth. He had pitched his second no-hitter of the season and, at last, he had discovered the joy of pitching a no-hitter . . . and winning.

With that game, Maloney became the first pitcher in baseball history to pitch two extra-inning no-hitters and the fourth to pitch two no-hitters in one season.

FOUR

BACK TO BACK

Johnny Vander Meer was almost too good to be believed. When he was seventeen, Hollywood made a movie about him even before he ever pitched a ball as a professional.

It was 1932 and the National League asked the film industry to make a baseball documentary about a typical American boy getting his first tryout with a major-league team. The film was designed to entice boys into a career in baseball.

"Find me a lad who has a modest background,"

instructed National League president, John Heydler, to Brooklyn Dodger business manager Dave Driscoll, who had been commissioned to locate a boy to play the part. "His people must be middle class, he must be clean-cut, religious and his father should have an industrial background."

Driscoll found John Samuel Vander Meer in Midland Park, New Jersey, the son of a stone mason who had come to this country from Holland. Driscoll knew a great deal about Vander Meer. He was a left-handed fireballer who pitched in a local church league, and the Dodgers had been keeping a close watch on him.

While John's dad knew very little about baseball and could offer no tangible help, he never discouraged the boy or deprived him of a chance to play ball. But it was with some reluctance that he permitted John to leave home to make the movie.

For Driscoll and the Dodgers, as well as for young Vander Meer, it presented an ideal opportunity. The boy would go to the Dodgers' spring training camp in Miami to film the picture and, at the same time, the Dodgers could look him over as a prospect.

Dodger manager Max Carey was not particularly impressed with the erratic left-hander and decided to send him back home to New Jersey without a contract when the film was completed. But Joe Shaute, a veteran left-handed pitcher who had taken a liking to Johnny, interceded. He pleaded with Carey to give the kid a chance, and the manager agreed to sign him and send him to Dayton, a Dodger farm team in Ohio.

In his first year of professional baseball at Dayton, Vandy won eleven and lost ten, a record that certainly indicated enough promise to warrant another chance.

However, Dayton manager Ducky Holmes thought not. The kid was too wild to suit Holmes who recommended John be released.

Confused and discouraged, Vander Meer returned to New Jersey to learn he had been purchased by Scranton, which was more confusing since Scranton was in a higher minor-league classification than Dayton. It wasn't until he arrived at Scranton that the mystery was solved. On the club was his old friend, Joe Shaute, who had been sold by Brooklyn to Cincinnati and then farmed out to Scranton.

Under Shaute's tutelage, Vander Meer showed good progress, so good in fact that Larry MacPhail, general manager of the Cincinnati Reds, purchased his contract for $4,000.

After an average year at Scranton, Cincinnati sold Vander Meer's contract to Boston, but MacPhail's interest was renewed when the young left-hander struck out 295 batters at Durham and was named minor leaguer of the year in 1936. This time, it cost MacPhail $10,000 of the Reds' money to get Vander Meer back in the Cincinnati organization.

At Syracuse in 1937, Vandy won only five and lost eleven, but Cincinnati manager Bill McKechnie called him up to the Reds late in the season and he posted a 3–5 record.

John was invited to spring training with the Reds in 1938, but he could find no reason for optimism. He had labored six seasons in the minor leagues to get there, but he arrived with very little hope of staying in the majors. He could throw hard but not accurately, a malady that has been the downfall of many promising pitchers.

It was McKechnie, the kindly, old Deacon of the

Reds, who gave Johnny his biggest boost one day in Lynchburg, Virginia. Vander Meer was pitching batting practice and McKechnie was leaning on the batting cage, giving the youngster the once-over. Suddenly, Johnny heard the Deacon shout excitedly, to no one in particular, "He's got it, he's got it! This boy's going to make it."

It made Johnny feel good, almost as good as he felt two months later when he shut out the New York Giants in the Polo Grounds. Now Johnny had confidence. He had promised himself that if he did not stick with the Reds in 1938, he would quit baseball and start in some other business. But those thoughts were far from his mind as he took his regular turn in the Cincinnati pitching rotation — a rookie on a staff that included such outstanding veteran pitchers as Paul Derringer, Bucky Walters, and Lee Grissom.

On June 11, he went out to face the Boston Bees. Johnny was particularly fast that day. He fired his fast ball past Boston hitters and in nine innings, not one of them could hit him safely. Johnny Vander Meer had pitched a no-hitter in his rookie season!

His next start was to be in Brooklyn against the Dodgers on June 15, and 38,748 fans turned out for the game — not just to see Johnny Vander Meer, although their curiosity had been raised by the flame-throwing rookie sensation.

The main attraction was New York's first night baseball game. MacPhail had introduced baseball under lights in Cincinnati in 1935, but the spectacle had been slow to catch on. When the energetic, imaginative Mac-Phail moved to Brooklyn, he took his midsummer night's dream with him.

Night baseball proved an immediate hit in Brooklyn; Vander Meer had to wait a few innings for his acceptance. By the third inning, however, the novelty of the lights had worn off and the fans settled down to watch the ball game. In the fourth, the Reds pushed across four runs and the interest centered on Vander Meer, who had yet to allow a hit.

Until 1938, seven pitchers had thrown two no-hitters, but none of them had pitched two in one season, let alone pitching them back-to-back. Baseball experts had a sound theory on why this was so. They contended that a no-hitter was a psychological and emotional drain on a pitcher and that it often took three or four starts for him to build himself up to a psychological peak again.

Vander Meer, however, was a rookie who had never heard of this theory. He simply kept mowing the Dodgers down, and as he prepared to face them in the ninth inning with a 6–0 lead the packed stands were in a frenzy of excitement and tension.

The first batter in the ninth was the veteran first baseman, Buddy Hassett. Buddy swung at the first pitch and sent a bouncer to the first-base side of the pitcher's mound. Vander Meer swept off the mound in a flash, scooped up the ball in his glove hand, and, in one continuous motion, tagged Hassett as he sped by.

The partisan Brooklyn fans, mixed with many of Johnny's friends and relatives from nearby New Jersey, cheered the young man on every pitch and moaned when he walked the next batter, Babe Phelps, on five pitches. Cookie Lavagetto also walked, bringing up the dangerous Dodger slugger, Dolph Camilli.

The first pitch to Camilli was a strike and the crowd cheered. But the cheers turned to boos when Brooklyn

manager, Burleigh Grimes, called time to send Goody
Rosen in as a runner for Phelps. It was good strategy, but
the Dodger fans were not interested in strategy at that
moment. They were not even interested in seeing their
heroes win the game. They wanted to see Johnny
Vander Meer pitch an historic second consecutive no-
hitter.

Play resumed and Vandy fired four straight balls,
walking Camilli and filling the bases with one out.
Cincinnati manager McKechnie called time and slowly
walked to the mound to have a talk with his young
pitcher. The fans knew he was not there to remove
Vander Meer because there was no Cincinnati pitcher
warming up in the bullpen. The Deacon had gone out
simply to try to settle his young pitcher.

"Heck, kid," McKechnie said, "they're more scared
of that ball than you are. Pour it in there."

Ernie Koy was the next batter and Vander Meer
poured in a strike. The next pitch was hit on the ground
to third, where Lew Riggs picked it up and, taking his
time, fired home to force Rosen. There was no time for
catcher Ernie Lombardi to double Koy at first.

The next hitter was the pesky competitor Leo
Durocher, known as one of the league's most dangerous
hitters in the pinch. Vandy threw a ball . . . then a
strike . . . then another strike. Leo swung viciously at
the next pitch, and the crowd groaned as the ball headed
on a sharp line into the right-field corner — then there
was a sigh of relief as the ball hooked foul.

Vandy put all he had into his next pitch, and
Durocher swung, lifting a high, lazy fly to center field.
Harry Craft moved in and took the ball easily, and
Johnny Vander Meer had made baseball history. He had

The immortal Babe Ruth was a spectator on the night Johnny Vander Meer (left) pitched his second straight no-hitter.

completed baseball's first back-to-back no-hitters. To make it even sweeter, in the stands were his mother, father, brother, sister, and fiancée. And there was the added irony that Vander Meer had spoiled Brooklyn's first night game for Larry MacPhail, who twice had purchased his contract for Cincinnati before moving over to the Dodgers.

News of Vander Meer's unique accomplishment was spread all over the country, even to the little town of San Dimas, California, where a tall, skinny right-hander for Bonita High School was attracting professional baseball scouts. On the same team was an outfielder who also attracted attention, but in another sport — Glenn Davis, who went to West Point to win fame as Mr. Outside to Doc Blanchard's Mr. Inside, possibly the greatest one-two running punch in college football history.

But Ewell Blackwell, a lanky six-foot, five-inch pitcher with a devastating sidearm motion, was the boy the baseball scouts were interested in at Bonita High. When he was graduated, the Dodgers tried to sign him to a contract. Blackie was interested, but he made one unusual demand: He would sign with the Dodgers if they permitted him to go to spring training with the big club. The Dodgers refused, and Blackwell passed up pro ball to enroll in California's LaVerne Teachers College on a basketball scholarship.

Along came the Cincinnati Reds with another contract offer. Again Blackwell repeated his demand to be allowed to go to spring training with the Reds. Cincinnati agreed, and Blackwell was signed to a contract with the Reds' Ogden, Utah, farm team. Blackwell never saw Ogden. As he had carefully planned, the Reds were so impressed with Ewell during the spring of 1942, they decided to keep him in the major leagues.

It was soon obvious that Blackwell was in over his head, so the Reds sent him to Syracuse, where he gained needed experience and terrorized International League batters, winning sixteen games during the regular season. In the play-offs, he won four games and chalked up thirty consecutive scoreless innings. An attack of pneumonia sidelined him for the Little World Series.

World War II interrupted Blackie's career for the next three seasons, but he returned to Cincinnati in 1946. Because he was late for spring training and had been out of competition for three years he managed to hang up only a 9-13 record. But he impressed National League hitters, who nicknamed him "The Whip," because of the whiplike motion he achieved when he brought his long, dangling arm around by way of third base.

"He pitches like a man falling out of a tree," said the veteran Dodger shortstop, PeeWee Reese, who meant it as a compliment.

By 1947, Blackwell was ready to win in the big leagues. He started slowly, showing a 2–2 record after the first month of the season, but as he faced the Boston Braves on the night of June 18, he had reeled off seven consecutive victories. Number eight was a classic. He set the Braves down without a hit!

Ever since Johnny Vander Meer pitched his back-to-back no-hitters in 1938, interest heightened whenever a pitcher went to the mound in his first start after pitching a no-hitter. Since Vandy's outstanding feat there had been nine no-hitters in the big leagues, but not one pitcher had been able to come close to doubling up. Now it was Ewell Blackwell, the tenth pitcher, trying to match Vander Meer.

In this case, the background for his attempt was marked by several startling coincidences. For one, both Vander Meer and Blackwell pitched for the Cincinnati Reds. For another, Vandy's no-hitters had come in the month of June nine years earlier. Blackwell's no-hitter was on June 18, and his next start would be on June 22 in Cincinnati.

Finally, Vander Meer's first no-hitter came against Boston and so had Blackwell's. Vandy's second was against the Dodgers and in his next start on June 22,

They called the Reds' Ewell Blackwell "The Whip" because of his unorthodox sweeping sidearm delivery.

Blackwell would be pitching against . . . the Brooklyn Dodgers.

A capacity crowd of 31,204 filled Cincinnati's Crosley Field on Sunday, June 22, 1947. It was the first game of a double-header, and the fans had come to see if Ewell Blackwell could make baseball lightning strike twice.

Vander Meer was still on the Cincinnati team, and his voice was the loudest as he leaned on the top step of the Reds' dugout shouting his encouragment as Blackwell calmly and effectively set the Dodgers down in the early innings.

For seven innings, Blackwell clung to a 1–0 lead and thrilled the crowd as he turned the Dodgers back without a hit. In the last of the eighth, the Reds scored three times and the outcome of the game was no longer in doubt. But the huge crowd sat tensely watching Blackie try to duplicate Vander Meer.

The first batter in the ninth was Gene Hermanski, pinch-hitting for pitcher Hank Behrman. Hermanski popped a short fly to left, an easy chance for Augie Galan.

That brought up Eddie Stanky, the fierce little competitor known as "The Brat" because he annoyed opponents with his peskiness at bat and in the field.

Stanky took the first pitch. On the second he swung and rifled a grounder through the center of the diamond. Because of his octopus-like windup and awkward follow-through, Blackwell never was in good position to field a ball. This time it was his undoing.

He reached down with his glove and tried to snatch at the ball, but he was not fast enough. The ball squirted through his legs, bounded over second base, and trickled into center field as second baseman Benny Zientara and shortstop Eddie Miller tried vainly to flag it down. It was a hit, clean and unquestioned, and it deprived Ewell Blackwell of joining Johnny Vander Meer's exclusive club and the crowd groaned its disappointment.

One out later, Jackie Robinson also singled which took a little of the sting out of Blackwell's failure . . . but only a little.

"It was my own fault I didn't get it," Blackwell said philosophically to sports writers who had gathered around his locker after the game. "I should have fielded Stanky's ball. If I was quicker I would have. And if I got that one, Robinson never would have come to bat and I would have had my no-hitter. I have only myself to blame."

There is much that is similar in the careers of Johnny Vander Meer and Ewell Blackwell. Both had delayed starts in their big-league life and both achieved their greatest success in their early years, pitching no-hitters and showing a world of promise. Both could throw extremely hard, but both suffered physical disabilities that prevented them from living up to that promise.

Blackwell had a kidney removed shortly after he won twenty-two and lost eight in 1947 and was never the same. After two bad years, he rallied to win thirty-three and lose thirty over the 1950 and 1951 seasons. But he slumped to 3–12 in 1952 and was sold to the New York Yankees. He pitched in five games in the stretch run of the 1952 season, winning his only decision and helping the Yankees clinch a pennant.

In 1953, Blackwell worked in eight games for the Yankees with a 2–0 record, but a sore arm sidelined him for the second half of the season. He tried to come back, but the arm still hurt, so he retired to run his automobile agency in Florida with a storehouse of memories. In nine big-league seasons, Blackwell won eighty-two games, more than 25 per cent of them in one season.

Vander Meer had a succession of arm problems and never did master his control trouble. In 1940, two years after he had reached baseball's summit, he was sent to the minor leagues. He returned to have a brief run of success, winning forty-nine games from 1941 to 1943 and, after two bad years, came back to win seventeen in 1948. But two years later, he was traded to the Chicago

Cubs and then to the Cleveland Indians. He finished his career with a major-league record of 119–121 and never came close to being the pitcher he was on those two June days in 1938.

Vander Meer finally did pitch his third no-hitter in 1952, but he pitched it for Tulsa in the Texas League. He pitched it against Beaumont, which was managed by Harry Craft, the same center fielder who had caught Leo Durocher's fly for the last out on his greatest day fourteen years before.

FIVE

BUMPER CROP

Baseball is a game played by hundreds of thousands of young Americans all over the country. It is a game played in huge cities and tiny hamlets, in organized Little Leagues and on vacant lots.

No matter where it is played, if there is a boy with the potential to play professional baseball, the major league scouts will find him. They will find him just as they found Bob Feller—at a time when scouts learned about young boys with baseball talent simply by being in the right place at the right time.

In 1935, the right place to be was on a wheat farm in the town of Van Meter, Iowa, population five hundred. Cy Slapnicka of the Cleveland Indians was there.

Robert William Andrew Feller had been born in Van Meter on November 3, 1918, the first offspring of Mr. & Mrs. William Feller. In his day, Bill Feller was a pretty good baseball player who never got beyond local semi-professional ranks. He dreamed often of someday having a son who would succeed in baseball where he had failed; and when Robert William Andrew came along, Bill Feller knew immediately that here was a fine young son to build a dream on.

The farm was neither very big nor very profitable, but there were always clothes to wear, food on the table, and a roof over their heads. And when the daily chores were done, there was always time for Bill and his son to have a catch. Bill Feller made certain of that.

It was during one of their nightly catches that Bill Feller came to a great decision. He was undecided whether to turn his son into the game's greatest shortstop or the best pitcher of all time. Bob was only eleven and he rifled a throw that tore through his father's glove, striking him in the side.

There was a mixed feeling of pain and pride, although at that moment, pain was the stronger feeling. Bob's throw had broken three of his father's ribs.

"From now on, Bob," Bill Feller announced, "you are a pitcher."

Saying it is one thing. Doing it is something else, and Bill Feller did something about it. He worked with Bob, teaching him how to throw a curve ball, making him practice every night to perfect his control. Bob pitched in grade school, then in American Legion ball;

79

he went on to Van Meter High School, where he became the team's best pitcher. In his sophomore year, he pitched five no-hitters.

And when the competition seemed inadequate for Bob's ability, Bill Feller did something about that, too. He formed his own team and built his own ball park.

Together he and his son cleared a field and built a diamond near the Raccoon River. They worked all spring to erect the ball park. They put up a scoreboard and wooden stands, then gathered the best players in Van Meter and neighboring towns and formed a team. The field was called Oakview Park and the team was named the Oakviews. Bill Feller was the manager, and Bob, naturally, was the star pitcher.

Two years later, Bob had outgrown his competition and moved to a top American Legion team in Des Moines, which won the state championship.

Bob Feller's reputation was now statewide, and he looked forward eagerly to the 1935 season when he would be competing against adults in fast semipro leagues. Bob was sixteen and pitching for the Farmers Union Insurance team of Des Moines with and against men almost twice his age. He had completed his junior year in Van Meter High and major league scouts were beginning to show up whenever he pitched. One day in July, Bob and his dad were working in the fields when a tall stranger approached them.

"Howdy," the stranger said, addressing Bob's father. "I'm Cyril Slapnicka of the Cleveland Indians. That the boy they tell me is quite a pitcher?"

"That's Bob, all right," Bill Feller said proudly.

"I'd like to see him pitch, Mr. Feller. When will he pitch again and where?"

"In Des Moines, day after tomorrow for the Farmers Union team," Bob heard his dad say.

"I'll be there," the man said, then waved good-by and walked off.

Bob pitched for the Farmers Union team as Cy Slapnicka watched. That night Slapnicka drove to the Feller home to have a talk with Bill Feller. When Slapnicka left, Bob learned his father had agreed to have him play the following spring with Fargo-Moorehead in North Dakota, a Cleveland farm team in the Northern League. Bob was too excited to sleep that night. "I'm on my way to the Cleveland Indians," he kept thinking.

But he never made it to Fargo-Moorehead. In April of 1936, he developed a sore arm and, in a panic, Bob's father wrote to Slapnicka.

"Don't let him throw a pitch," Slapnicka replied. "I'll send for him soon."

For the first time in his young life, Bob sat on the sidelines, his heart breaking, as he watched the Van Meter High team play that spring. It should have been his biggest year; but there he was, a seventeen-year-old pitcher with a sore arm, not knowing if he would ever be able to pitch again . . . and, if he did, not knowing if his fast ball would still have the usual steam to it.

In June, the call came from Slapnicka and Bob packed his bags and headed for Cleveland for treatment on his arm. He worked out carefully under Slapnicka's supervision, throwing lightly with Bruce Campbell, the Indians' regular right fielder. Campbell had been left in Cleveland when the club went on an extended eastern trip because he was recovering from an attack of spinal meningitis.

Slowly, aided by the heat and exercise, Bob could

feel the strength returning to his arm. One day he cut loose his best fast ball and Campbell winced and shouted, "Hey, kid, take it easy. I'm an outfielder, not a catcher." Bob knew his fast ball had returned.

The Indians arranged to have the youngster pitch a game for the Rosenblums, a local semipro outfit. He pitched a 3–2, twelve-inning victory and when he returned to the clubhouse after the game, he was greeted by Slapnicka, who had been a most interested spectator.

"You looked great kid. Now I've got a surprise for you. The Indians play the Cardinals next week in an exhibition game. You're going to pitch against them."

Pitch against the St. Louis Cardinals! Bob could hardly believe his ears — he could hardly control his excitement. The famous Gashouse Gang with Frank Frisch, Pepper Martin, Dizzy Dean, Terry Moore, Joe Medwick, Leo Durocher! It was too good to be true.

But it was true. On July 6, at Cleveland's League Park, with 10,000 people in the stands, Bob Feller, seventeen years, eight months, and three days old, walked out of the bullpen to start the fourth inning.

He fired his warmup pitches to catcher-manager Steve O'Neill, while the Cardinals looked on with curiosity at the young phenom.

"Hey, Stu," said Cardinal manager and second baseman Frank Frisch to utility infielder Stu Martin after watching Feller throw, "you play for me. I don't feel well."

The first batter was catcher Bruce Ogrodowski and Bob pumped into his windup, reared back, and fired his fast one straight and true into O'Neill's big mitt. He heard the loud crack echo through the ball park and he heard the umpire screech, "steeerrikke one."

82

In 1938, at age 19, Cleveland's Bob Feller won 17 games and struck out a record 18 Tiger batters in one game.

Now the nervousness began to disappear and he pitched again. A bunt . . . and Ogrodowski was thrown out at first. He had retired the first man he faced. He was in the big leagues.

The next batter, Leo Durocher, went down on strikes and so did Art Garibaldi. It was an easy start . . . almost too easy.

In the fifth, Feller got his third straight strikeout and now he was full of confidence and the crowd, quiet for four innings, began to come alive with the wonder of what was happening. But Terry Moore stroked a hit that unsettled Feller, and the young pitcher followed that with a walk to Stu Martin. Moore and Martin worked a double steal and in his haste to make a throw, O'Neill let the ball get through him for a passed ball, Moore scoring and Martin going to third.

Now the great Pepper Martin came to bat, and Feller put everything he had into the next three pitches. Martin missed all three. Rip Collins was next and became the kid's fifth strikeout victim.

In the sixth, he struck out all three hitters. It was a sparkling performance for one so young. He faced eleven batters, struck out eight, and allowed one hit and one walk. The papers the next day were lavish in their praise for the young fireballer just off an Iowa farm.

A photographer grabbed Bob and dragged him to the Cardinal dugout, then called out to the great Dizzy Dean.

"Hey, Diz," the cameraman shouted, "how about posing for a picture with the kid?"

"If it's all right with him, it's all right with me," said the good-natured Dizzy. "After what he did out there, he's the guy to say."

Young Bob was in the clouds as he dashed to his hotel after the game to telephone his dad. Bob's enthusiasm was tempered by his dad's caution.

"That's fine, Bob," he said, "but it was only an exhibition game. It might not be so easy during a regulation game."

Technically, Bob was not yet a member of the Indians, but the paperwork was soon completed and he was placed on the roster. He spent his first few weeks sitting with the veteran catcher, Wally Schang, who passed along vital pitching tips and told him how to pitch to each American League hitter. Bob devoured the information ravenously.

On July 19, Bob Feller got into an official major-league game for the first time. It was the second game of a double-header in Washington. He pitched one inning, walked a man, hit another, and struck out one, but he did not allow a hit.

He worked a few more games in relief, watching the Indians fade out of contention for the American League pennant and growing impatient for his chance. It came, finally, on August 23, 1936, in Cleveland against the St. Louis Browns.

It was a debut that may never be matched. At least it will never be forgotten. Bob won the game, 4–1, but that was not the big news. He struck out fifteen batters, one short of the American League record, two short of the major-league record, and the most strikeouts in a single game by an American League pitcher since Bob Shawkey fanned fifteen in 1919, when Feller was just a few months old. The baseball world was astonished by this sensational first start by a kid who still had not reached his eighteenth birthday.

His proud father (right), and his discoverer, Cy Slapnicka, look on as Bob Feller signs his first Cleveland contract.

Three starts later, on September 13, Bob pitched against the Philadelphia Athletics. He struck out seventeen batters to break the American League record and tie Dizzy Dean's major-league mark. Bob Feller was on his way. He finished with a record of 5–3 and the promise of future greatness although still a high school student.

But he was a famous high school student, a major-league pitcher who traveled around the country and got his picture in the newspapers. It was difficult concentrating on his studies that winter as he kept thinking about spring training and getting started on his first full season in the big leagues.

In February, he packed his bags and headed for Hot Springs, Arkansas, where he was to attend a baseball school. He had just turned eighteen and there was still much to learn before he could be considered an accomplished major-league pitcher.

Wherever the Indians played that spring, huge crowds came out to see the boy wonder and visiting newspapermen cast a critical eye in his direction. Rarely had one so young crashed the major-league scene with such a flourish.

But Bob's joy was short-lived. Three weeks after the season started he had a recurrence of his arm trouble and doctors advised him to rest. It was to be two months before he pitched again, but he used the time to good advantage. He went home to Van Meter to earn his high school diploma.

Graduation day was like nothing they had ever seen in Van Meter. It was covered by the press and his classmates made a papier-mâché baseball in which the diplomas were placed. They unveiled a picture of Bob Feller in a baseball uniform and even called upon the boy hero to make a speech.

It was an unforgettable day, but Bob was anxious to get back to Cleveland to resume his baseball career. With the help of a chiropractor, Bob's sore arm was cured; but he went through a frustrating time, losing his first four games.

Then things began to turn. On August 25, he struck out sixteen Red Sox and he finished the season winning nine of his last twelve decisions to salvage the season with a 9–7 record. More important, he was beginning to feel as if he belonged. He looked forward to a fresh start in 1938, when he would take his turn in the Indians' starting rotation.

It was the year that would firmly establish Bob Feller as one of the game's top pitchers, not merely a young man with a world of promise. The Indians lost the opening game of the season, 6–2, to the St. Louis Browns, and Feller got the call to pitch the second game in Cleveland's League Park.

He zipped through the first five innings without allowing a hit and he faced catcher Billy Sullivan to start the sixth. Bob's first pitch was a crackling curve ball and his momentum carried him toward first base. Sullivan bunted the ball to the third-base side of the pitcher's mound. Bob straightened up, changed direction, pounced on the ball, and fired it hard to first base; but the speedy Sullivan beat the throw by half a step. It was a sad way to lose a no-hitter, and some reporters were critical of Sullivan for bunting his way on.

"It was only the sixth inning and we were behind by four runs," explained Sullivan, who had been a teammate of Feller's in Cleveland. "We still had a chance to win and that's why I bunted. I thought I might start a rally. I like to see any pitcher turn in a no-hit game. It helps baseball. Would I have done it in the ninth inning? I probably would. There's no use cheapening a no-hitter by giving up."

Bob won seventeen games and lost eleven that year, and on October 2, in his last start of the season, he struck out eighteen Detroit Tigers, breaking Dizzy Dean's major-league record. In his previous start, he had ten strikeouts and the twenty-eight in two successive games was also a record.

By 1939, Bob was a full-fledged star. He led the American League pitchers with twenty-four victories, and was named to open the 1940 season against the Chicago White Sox on April 16 at Comiskey Park.

It was a raw, gusty day, the kind that makes it difficult for a pitcher to loosen his arm muscles. Feller did not have his usual overpowering stuff, but he dueled Edgar Smith for three scoreless innings, until the Indians put over a run in the fourth.

The score was 1–0 and that is how it remained into the ninth. Feller had not allowed a hit and he quickly disposed of the first two batters and prepared to face Luke Appling, one of the toughest hitters in the game. Appling could always be depended upon to get a piece of the ball and he practically wore Feller down, fouling off ten pitches before taking ball four. The next batter was Taft Wright, a strong left-handed hitter.

The first pitch was a fast ball inside and Wright swung and lashed a sharp ground ball between first and second. Ray Mack, the Indians' second baseman, ranged far to his left toward the right-field grass. He stumbled momentarily and Feller held his breath; but Mack recovered his footing, scooped up the ball, and threw Wright out by two strides. Bob Feller had pitched the first Opening Day no-hitter in baseball history!

Bob went on from there to win fifty-two games in the next two seasons. He was the acknowledged king of major-league pitchers. Players and fans spoke with awe about his blazing fast ball, which was timed at the speed of 100 miles per hour. Old-timers argued about whether Bob was faster than Walter Johnson, the famous "Big Train," who was said to have thrown a baseball faster than any man who ever lived. Feller had his supporters, however, and with his best years still ahead of him at the age of twenty-three, experts predicted that he would erase many records, that he would be a cinch to win thirty games one year and take his place alongside the game's outstanding pitchers.

But on December 7, 1941, the Japanese bombed Pearl Harbor, throwing the United States into World War II. Two days later, Bob Feller enlisted in the United States Navy. It would be 44 months before he

89

resumed his career.

During the war, Feller earned eight battle stars; and finally, in August of 1945, he came marching back to baseball amid doubt and skepticism that he could regain the Feller form of old after having missed almost four seasons.

A crowd of 46,477 welcomed Feller back to Cleveland and he responded by beating the Tigers, 4–2, in his first game, striking out twelve and erasing most of the doubt.

There were only six weeks left in the season and Bob worked in only nine games, but a special post-season exhibition tour put him into shape for the 1946 season, when most of the players had returned from war.

To Feller went the honor of pitching the 1946 season opener against the Chicago White Sox, which resulted in a satisfying 1–0 victory. But when he lost his next two games, rumors began to spread about Feller's future. Members of the press wondered in big, black headlines if Bob had come to the end of the line. He was only twenty-seven, an age when a pitcher is usually at the peak of his career. But he had lost four full seasons of competition while in the Navy. Such a lay-off has been known to dull a pitcher's skills.

By the time the Indians reached New York to meet the Yankees on April 30, Feller was beginning to wonder if the reporters saw something he could not see. His arm felt strong and he thought he was throwing as well as he ever did, but it did not show in the results.

He was a determined pitcher as he went out to face the Yankees that day. He started the game by getting Phil Rizzuto and George Stirnweiss on ground balls, then he walked Tommy Henrich and got Joe DiMaggio

The classic confrontation between super-stars: Bob Feller pitching, Joe DiMaggio batting. Bob emerged with no-hitter.

to force Henrich at second. It was an easy inning, but the Feller trademark — the strikeout — was missing.

In the second, he found his strikeout pitch, getting Nick Etten and Joe Gordon on strikes after Charlie Keller had led off the inning with a walk. When Keller was thrown out attempting to steal, Feller had completed two hitless innings.

Bill Dickey walked to open the third, but Bob got pitcher Bill Bevens, Rizzuto, and Stirnweiss on strikes. Again, in the fourth, he walked the first man, Henrich, then got DiMaggio on a pop, and struck out the next two.

By the fifth inning, the huge Yankee Stadium crowd of 37,144, which had come out of nostalgia and curiosity, began to swing to Bob's side. They had come to see for themselves if the stories of his demise were true and they stayed to cheer him on as he ended the fifth by making Dickey and Bevens his eighth and ninth strikeout victims.

He got by the sixth inning without another strikeout, but he still had not allowed a hit, and in the seventh he added another strikeout in a 1–2–3 inning. Strikeout number eleven was sandwiched between two ground balls in the eighth and the tension was oppressive as Bob prepared to start the ninth inning. In the top half, Cleveland catcher Frankie Hayes had hit into the left-field seats to produce the game's only run and Bob walked with that jaunty gait of his to the center of the diamond to protect his lead.

Stirnweiss' bouncer to first was booted for an error to open the ninth, the kind of break on which the Yankees inevitably capitalized. Henrich sacrificed and the fearsome Joe DiMaggio batted. Joe was a fierce competitor for Feller, running the count to 3–2 and fouling off pitch after agonizing pitch. Finally, he drove a ball to shortstop and Lou Boudreau made the play and threw him out. One man to go . . . Charlie Keller.

Feller pitched and the ball was a high, easy, chopping grounder hit directly at second baseman Ray Mack, who charged it quickly. But as he did, he stumbled and fell to his knees — the crowd let out a gasp of disappointment. But somehow, Mack managed to get the ball in his glove, scramble to his feet, and throw out the speeding Keller by a step. Bob Feller had pitched his second no-hitter!

It was sweet revenge for Feller in the face of reports he was finished and he could hardly help crowing to reporters. "I threw very few curve balls," he said. "I wanted to prove I could throw as hard as ever."

It was his greatest game and set the tempo for what was to be his greatest season. He finished with twenty-six victories and established an all-time record by striking out 348 batters.

Bob followed that up with twenty victories in 1947 and nineteen in 1948 as the Indians won their first American League pennant in twenty-eight years. Feller was going to realize a lifetime dream, he was going to pitch in the World Series.

He pitched the opening game of the 1948 World Series against the Boston Braves, but he lost, 1–0, to Johnny Sain. Bob got one more chance, in the fifth game, but he was pounded hard. His failure to win a World Series game was his one regret when he retired some years later.

Feller tailed off in 1949, winning only fifteen and losing fourteen and the following year he won sixteen and lost eleven. Once again, they were writing that the end had come — and this time it had more credibility since Bob had passed the age of thirty-two. But his competitive urge would not permit him to go down without a fight and he made one more remarkable stand.

In 1951, he fired the Cleveland team that battled the Yankees to the wire for the American League pennant. The Yankees won, but Bob won twenty-two and lost only eight. One of the victories was Bob's third no-hitter, against the Detroit Tigers on July 1. Only Lawrence J. Corcoran, before the turn of the century, and Cy Young, in the era of the dead ball, had pitched three no-hitters before Feller.

But 1951 was Bob's last good year, for in 1952, he suffered through the first losing season of his career, winning nine and losing thirteen. He remained a valuable part-time pitcher for the Indians over the next three seasons, winning twenty-seven and losing fourteen, but he called it quits after 1956, a year in which he was 0–4 at age thirty-seven.

It had been an illustrious career. Bob Feller had won 266 games, lost 162, struck out 2,581 batters, and pitched three no-hitters; but the statistics hardly tell the story of the man many consider to be the greatest fireballer of all time. He had missed four seasons at the height of his career, and there is no telling what his record might have been had World War II not robbed him of those peak years.

His most staggering achievement is the number of one-hit games Feller pitched — twelve of them, five more than any other pitcher in history — a record that may never be equalled. Even Sandy Koufax, who pitched four no-hitters, pitched only two one-hitters. If a no-hitter is luck, then a one-hitter is an absence of luck; and with a little bit of luck, Bob Feller might have pitched seven or eight no-hitters.

A batter's view of Bob Feller's curve ball, caught in nine positions by the magic of the camera.

ONCE IN A LIFETIME

Marichal...Burdette...Maglie...Wilhelm...Johnson...
Marquard...Vance...Hubbell...P. Dean...Lemon...

One For Juan

In Houston, Texas, on a hot and humid June 15, 1963, B.D. (before the dome), Juan Marichal of the San Francisco Giants was warming up for a start against the Astros when first baseman Willie McCovey ambled by.

"Hey, Weelie," said Marichal. "Tonight I do something different. I change my windup and use my number two motion. What do you think?"

"I think you must be nuts," McCovey replied. "You just won five games in a row and you shut out Los Angeles four days ago. Why change?"

95

"Because Houston hit me pretty good last time," Marichal argued, "and I had good stuff. Maybe they have figured out my motion. This time I give them something else."

What Marichal did was simply bring his hands to his belt instead of winding up before pitching. Normally

The Giants' Juan Marichal hinted of a bright future when he threw a one-hitter in his first major league start.

he dipped deeply and kicked high before delivering, but he suspected that gave the Astros time to see his grip on the ball and read his pitches. By abandoning the windup he was reducing the time between pitches. With his new delivery, Marichal beat the Astros, 1–0, and pitched the first no-hitter by a Giant in thirty-four years.

That was the year that marked the coming of Juan Marichal and stamped him as the outstanding young right-handed pitcher in baseball. He led the National League with 25 victories, worked a league high of 321 innings, struck out 248 batters, and posted a 2.41 earned run average.

Marichal had to wait four years for his first major-league no-hitter. That may not seem a long time, yet it once appeared Juan would not have to wait more than a day to enter the pitchers' hall of fame.

Juan Antonio Marichal, born in Laguna Verde, the Dominican Republic, was playing service ball while in his country's air force when the Giants spotted him. They signed him for $500 and sent him to Michigan City in the Midwest League to begin his professional career in 1958.

With his high kick and flaming fast ball, Juan was an instant sensation as he won twenty-one games. Although only twenty years old and unable to say more than two or three words in English, he proved he could pitch. The following year, at Springfield in the Eastern League, he won eighteen and in 1960 he was sent to Tacoma, the Giants' top farm.

By July, Marichal had won eleven games when the Giants summoned him to San Francisco. For ten days, he did nothing but pitch batting practice. Then, on July 19, manager Bill Rigney handed him the ball and sent him out to make his major-league debut against the Philadelphia Phillies.

Marichal struck out the first two hitters he faced. As he entered the eighth inning he still had not allowed a hit, unaware that never in the history of modern baseball had a pitcher pitched a no-hitter in his first major league appearance. History was foiled when Clay Dalrymple pinch hit a single with two out in the eighth, but that was the only hit the Phillies got off Marichal, who struck out twelve in the 2–0 victory.

A Hand-To-Mouth Existence

He stands on the mound, the picture of grim determination. He is nervous and fidgety, prancing around, pawing at the dirt with his spikes, hiking his trousers from the belt, adjusting his cap. In one quick, sudden motion his pitching hand darts to his mouth; then he flashes it against the front of his uniform shirt. He bends over to take the sign from his catcher, then swings into his windup in that quick rocking chair motion of his, and fires the ball with such force he falls off the mound.

He is Lou Burdette, and for almost two decades he has been one of the toughest, most competitive pitchers in baseball. He also has been one of the most controversial. The reason for the controversy is his habit of putting his hand to his mouth.

When he does, rival managers and players charge "spitter." The spitball has been illegal for thirty years, but for fifteen years Burdette has been accused of throwing one. While opponents made accusations, Burdette remained silent. He never said he did, but he never said he didn't.

"Let them think I throw it," Burdette said. "That gives me an edge because it's another pitch they have to worry about."

For all his success, Lou Burdette is another of the many pitchers who got his no-hitter at an advanced age. He was almost thirty-four and his best years were behind him when Lou faced the Philadelphia Phillies on August 18, 1960. He held the Phillies hitless, winning a 1–0 thriller amid the inevitable charge that he was using a "wet one."

While the no-hitter was a great thrill, Burdette's biggest moment came three years earlier in the 1957 World Series against the New York Yankees. He won

Opposing batters often accused Lou Burdette of throwing a spitball and this picture indicates why.

the second game, 4–2, to tie the Series at one game apiece; and he blanked the Yankees, 1–0, in the fifth game to give the Milwaukee Braves a 3–2 lead in games.

The Yankees won the sixth game and for the deciding seventh game, manager Fred Haney gave the ball to Burdette. Pitching with only two days' rest, Lou beat the Yankees, 5–0, showing his usual courage and determination. It was his third World Series victory and his second consecutive shutout as he pitched Milwaukee to the top of the baseball world.

The drama of the game was over-emphasized because in 1951, just six years earlier, Burdette had been a promising young pitcher owned by the Yankees and playing in the Triple A Pacific Coast League.

Anxious to obtain a veteran relief pitcher to help them insure the pennant, the Yankees obtained Johnny Sain from the Braves. The price was $50,000, but the Braves would not okay the deal unless the Yankees threw in a young pitcher to replace Sain. The Yankees agreed and the throw-in pitcher was a young man named Lou Burdette.

A Close Shave

Sinister-looking Sal Maglie owned the Dodgers. Oh, he wasn't a stockholder of the Brooklyn baseball club, but when he pitched for the New York Giants from 1950 to 1955, they used to say that all Sal had to do was throw his glove on the mound and the Dodgers would roll over and die.

In those six years, Maglie, nicknamed "The Barber" because he shaved the batters closely, won twenty-two games from the Dodgers.

It was a long, hard road that Sal Maglie took to the major leagues. He signed his first professional contract with Buffalo in 1938 and after five hard years he had made no progress in baseball. He sat out the 1943 and 1944 seasons to work in a defense plant during World War II and returned to baseball in 1945 with Jersey City. Later that year he was called up by the Giants, posting a 5–4 record.

Sal was twenty-nine years old with very little future in the spring of 1946 when opportunity knocked. The Mexican League made a generous offer and Sal jumped to the outlaw league hoping to gain fame and fortune. However, after two years, the Mexican League was defunct and Maglie returned to the United States to discover he and the other jumpers were banned from playing professional ball in the States.

Finally, in 1950 the ban was lifted and Maglie was taken back by the Giants. He had never been much of a pitcher, and at the age of thirty-three he was so lightly regarded he spent most of the early weeks of the season on the bench.

When his chance came, Maglie made the most of it. In Mexico he had developed an outstanding curve ball and learned how to vary it in speed and the size of its break to keep hitters off balance. Almost overnight he became the sensation of the National League, winning eighteen and losing only four.

The following year he was 23–6 and the year after that he had an 18–8 record. But his age and a chronic back problem worked against him and, in 1955, the Giants sold him to the Cleveland Indians. He did not win a game for them, and it looked like Maglie had come to the end of the line when, on May 15, 1956, the

Sal Maglie, who pitched a no-hitter for the Dodgers in 1956, lost to Don Larsen's perfect game in World Series that year.

Indians put him up for sale.

Only one team was willing to take a chance on him. It was his old nemesis, the Brooklyn Dodgers. Desperately in need of pitching help, the Dodgers decided to gamble on Sal's arm and head. They hoped he would regain some of his old magic by being back in the familiar National League.

Jackie Robinson (left) and Gil Hodges exult with Maglie after Sal beat the Yankees in the opening game of 1956 Series.

The gamble proved to be worthwhile. In four months, Maglie won eleven and lost five, helping to keep the Dodgers in the pennant race as they came barreling into the final week of the season battling neck and neck with the Milwaukee Braves. With five games remaining, the two teams were tied as they began play on September 25.

The Braves beat Cincinnati in the afternoon to take a temporary half game lead as the Dodgers faced Philadelphia at night. Manager Walt Alston sent Maglie to the mound to try to keep pace with the Braves. The Barber not only won the game, 5–0, but he pitched the first no-hitter of his career. At age thirty-nine, he became the oldest man to pitch a no-hitter since forty-one-year-old Cy Young pitched one in 1908.

Three days later Maglie and Clem Labine won a double-header against the Pittsburgh Pirates to clinch the Dodgers' second consecutive National League pennant.

Maglie was Alston's choice to open the World Series against the New York Yankees and he survived a rocky start to win, 6–3.

With the Series tied two games apiece, Alston again called on Maglie for the important fifth game. Old Sal pitched expertly, holding the Yankees to two runs and five hits. It was a performance that would have been good enough to win most days, but not that day. For on that day, Don Larsen pitched the first perfect game in World Series history.

Baseballs And Butterflies

James Hoyt Wilhelm always had a habit of finishing

what others started. James Hoyt Wilhelm is a relief
pitcher. There is no man in baseball who gets less
acclaim, yet is more valuable, than the relief pitcher.
The starting pitcher gets all the headlines and most of
the money. He can win twenty games or he can earn
lasting fame by pitching a no-hitter. But the relief
pitcher is a pitching staff's forgotten man — to everybody except the manager.

Relief pitching is a thankless job. A starting pitcher
works every fourth day. He knows when he will pitch
and he can prepare for that day. A relief pitcher is always
on call and he must be ready to pitch within moments
after that call. Usually when he enters the game it is at a

Knuckleballer Hoyt Wilhelm came out of the bullpen to pitch
a no-hitter when it seemed his career was coming to an end.

most crucial point. It is late in the game and there are runners on base and one mistake can cost a ball game. If he makes that mistake it is remembered. If he does not, it is forgotten; he is only doing his job.

The picture of a baseball fireman is one of a man striding in from the bullpen to fire fast balls past hitters in tight situations. Wilhelm does it with a tantalizing, baffling knuckleball, so perplexing a pitch it almost drove him out of the major leagues — not because it is easy to hit but because it is difficult to catch.

Wilhelm came up to the New York Giants in 1952, a comparatively old rookie of twenty-eight. He appeared in 71 games, won 15, lost only 3, had an earned run average of 2.43, and drove hitters and catchers crazy.

It became commonplace to see catchers don a mask just to warm him up in the bullpen. After five seasons with the Giants, Wilhelm and his butterfly were considered more of a liability than an asset and he was traded to the St. Louis Cardinals, where he won only one game and was sold to the Cleveland Indians within the year.

It was the same story in Cleveland, and less than a year later he was sold to the Baltimore Orioles. Hoyt Wilhelm and his knuckleball seemed to have come to the end of the line.

In desperate need of starting pitchers, Baltimore manager Paul Richards took Wilhelm out of the bullpen for the first time in his major-league life.

Retirement was in his mind when Wilhelm went to the mound to face the New York Yankees on September 20, 1958. He had won only two games all season and the future was far from bright for the thirty-five-year-old knuckleballer.

It was a cool, rainy day as Wilhelm dueled Don Larsen of perfect game fame. But this time it was Wilhelm's turn to be perfect . . . almost. Pitching for survival, he set the Yankees down without a hit and earned a new lease on his baseball life.

Wilhelm won fifteen games as a starter in 1959, then was returned to the bullpen where his value was greatest. It was stage two of Wilhelm's amazing career. Once again he became the terror of baseball with his knuckleball, tantalizing batters and catchers and frightening weak managers in crucial situations.

Once, Wilhelm got beaten in the ninth inning by a home run. Richards was fuming as he approached catcher Gus Triandos.

"What did you call for?" Richards inquired.

"His fast ball," Triandos replied.

"His fast ball," Richards exploded. "He hasn't got a fast ball. Why didn't you call for the knuckler?"

"I can't catch the darn thing," Triandos explained.

"If you can't catch it," Richards thundered, "don't you think the guy who hit that home run would have a harder time hitting it?"

On The Right Track

For thirteen years, Walter Perry Johnson had been baseball's supreme pitcher. The Big Train, as he was nicknamed because his fast ball reminded opponents of a runaway express, had done it all.

In 1908, he pitched three shutouts in four days. In 1910, he pitched a one-hitter and beat Eddie Plank and the Philadelphia Athletics on opening day as President William Howard Taft initiated a custom that still stands by throwing out the first ball.

In 1912, he won twelve consecutive games. In 1913, he won thirty-six games, lost only seven, and had a consecutive scoreless streak of fifty-six innings.

From 1910 through 1919 he won twenty or more games every year. He had reached the top of his profession, but as he entered his fourteenth year in 1920, Walter Johnson had not done the thing every pitcher dreams of doing. He had not pitched a no-hitter.

Johnson did not expect to be the Washington Senator pitcher when he arrived at Boston's Fenway Park an hour before game time on July 1, 1920. He had asked for, and received, permission to arrive late so that he might stay at home a little longer to be with his son, five-year-old Walter, Jr., who was seriously ill.

But when Walter arrived at Fenway, manager Clark Griffith asked if he would pitch and he agreed. He held the Red Sox hitless and allowed only one man to reach base safely — Harry Hooper made it on an error by second baseman Bucky Harris. Harris atoned for his

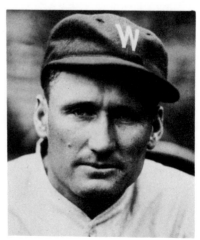

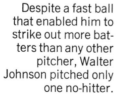

Despite a fast ball that enabled him to strike out more batters than any other pitcher, Walter Johnson pitched only one no-hitter.

107

error, however, by driving in the game's only run with a seventh-inning single.

Anxious to capitalize on Johnson's performance, Griffith announced that the big pitcher would make his next start on July 4 against Babe Ruth and the New York Yankees. Johnson never made it. He developed a sore arm which caused him not only to miss the assignment, but to post his poorest record in fourteen years, eight won and ten lost.

People said Johnson, at age thirty-three, had reached the end; but he came back in 1921 to win seventeen games and three years later, at the age of thirty-six, he won twenty-three games.

It is unusual for a man called "the greatest fast ball pitcher of all time," to have thrown only one no-hitter. Possibly it was because he had such exceptional control and hitters never feared for their safety when Johnson was pitching. They knew they could take a toe hold at the plate.

Unlike most pitchers of his generation, Johnson never experimented with the unpredictable spitball and he never intentionally threw at a batter. He got the job done by simply firing his fast ball past the batter.

In twenty-one big league seasons, Walter Johnson won 414 games, pitched a record 113 shutouts, and struck out a record 3,497 batters, proving that when you are good you do not need gimmicks to help you win.

As Luck Would Have It

Baseball players are, and always have been, a most superstitious lot. Although there is a great deal of proof to the contrary, some even think it is bad luck for a

Fashionable Rube Marquard pitched a no-hitter for the Giants in his first start of the 1915 season; by mid-year he was a Dodger.

pitcher to pitch a no-hitter.

"A pitcher is never the same after he pitches a no-hitter," they reason, without very much logic supporting the theory.

One such superstitious fellow was Richard William Marquard, nicknamed Rube because he could throw a smoking fast ball like Rube Waddell. Purchased by the New York Giants from Indianapolis in 1908 for $11,000, a staggering sum at the time, Marquard won only nine games and lost eighteen in his first three seasons. He became known as the "$11,000 lemon."

But, in 1911, he began to show he was well worth the price. He had a 24–7 record and followed it up in 1912 by running off a record nineteen consecutive victories.

The day after he won number nineteen, Marquard celebrated by treating himself to a present — a beautiful stickpin with a cluster of opals. Three days later he was beaten by Chicago, ending the streak, and as he dressed after the game a teammate noticed the stickpin.

"Hey, Rube," he said, "that's why you lost today. Don't you know opals are unlucky?"

Marquard marched right down to the river and threw his stickpin into the water. But the damage had been done, and for the remainder of the season he won only seven games and lost ten.

The following season, Rube won more than twenty games for the third consecutive year, posting a 23–10 record, but in 1914 he fell to a 12–22 record.

In his first game in 1915, on April 15, Marquard pitched a no-hitter, beating the Dodgers, 2–0. It was to be his last effective game of the season and the superstitious ones nodded.

By mid-season, the Giants released him and he was picked up by the Brooklyn Dodgers. In 1916, his first full year in Brooklyn, Marquard made a remarkable comeback. He won thirteen games and helped the Dodgers win their first National League pennant. In subsequent seasons he went on to win eighty-three more games for Brooklyn, Cincinnati, and Boston, finishing his career with 201 victories.

He Kept His Promise

Dazzy Vance came out of the Iowa farmlands with a blazing fast ball, a tattered shirt sleeve on his pitching arm, and a high-kicking left foot that threw hitters off their timing.

Arthur Charles Vance got his nickname because, as a boy, he tried to say "daisy" and it came out "dazzy."

An uncle tagged him with the name and it stuck. Years later it was natural for baseball people to call him "The Dazzler," which he was on the pitcher's mound.

For ten years Vance had banged around the minor leagues, looking for a break and being hindered by a sore arm. He had three brief trials in the big leagues — once with Pittsburgh and twice with the New York Yankees — and failed to win a big-league game, much less a big-league job, all three times.

Finally, after an operation on his pitching elbow, Vance was signed by Wilbert Robinson for the Brooklyn Dodgers in 1922. At the age of thirty-one, Dazzy Vance won his first big-league game. He won eighteen that year and soon established himself as one of the outstanding pitchers of his day.

Vance pitched until he was forty-four years old. When he finally retired, he had won 197 big-league games. He was a twenty-two game winner for the Dodgers at the age of thirty-seven, a seventeen-game winner at thirty-nine, and a twelve-game winner at forty-one.

In 1924, three years after he joined the Dodgers, Vance won twenty-eight games and lost only six. In 1925, he had a 22–9 record for a sixth-place team that won only sixty-eight games. It was in that year that Dazzy made the pitchers' hall of fame with a no-hitter right after a near miss.

In the first game of a double-header on September 8, Dazzy kicked his left leg high, waved his tattered shirt sleeve, and buzzed his blistering fast ball past the Philadelphia Phillies with ease. Only one man reached base against him. In the second inning, Chicken Hawks, the Philadelphia first baseman, hit a soft Texas Leaguer over

After pitching a one-hitter against the Phils, Dodger Dazzy
Vance said he'd get 'em on a no-hitter next time. He did.

the second baseman's head for the only hit off Vance. Hawks was thrown out attempting to steal second, and Vance faced the minimum twenty-seven batters, narrowly missing a perfect game.

"You lucky stiff," shouted Phillie manager Art Fletcher. "You won't pitch a one-hitter next time."

"Next time," boasted the outspoken Vance, "you won't even get one hit."

The next time was five days later, on September 13, in Brooklyn and again Vance worked the first game of a double-header. The Phillies scored early on Dazzy . . . but without a hit. A two-base error by the left fielder, an infield out, and a sacrifice fly brought home the Philadelphia run but that was all they got. The Dodgers won the game, 10–1, and true to his word, Dazzy Vance held the Phillies without a hit.

The Straight Ticket

The late Governor Alfred E. Smith of New York never made the White House, but he did make the baseball Hall of Fame . . . at least indirectly.

Edward Kinsella, a New York Giant scout and Illinois politician, had gone to the Democratic national convention in Houston, Texas, in 1928 to cast his delegation's vote for Governor Smith as the party's presidential nominee. During a lull at the convention, Kinsella decided to slip out to watch a baseball game between Houston and Beaumont of the Texas League.

Kinsella saw a long, lean, lanky left-hander named Carl Owen Hubbell beat Houston for Beaumont, 1–0 in eleven innings. Kinsella returned to his hotel and put in a call to Giant manager John McGraw strongly recom-

In his second year in the majors, 1929, Carl Hubbell threw a no-hitter. His greatest achievement, however, came five years later.

mending he sign Hubbell for the Giants. McGraw consented and Hubbell joined the Giants a few weeks later.

Kinsella did not know it at the time, but he had cast his vote with a winner — in Hubbell if not in Smith.

Nicknamed "The Meal Ticket" because he was the pitcher the Giants called on when they needed to win an important game, Hubbell pitched in the major leagues for sixteen years — all with the Giants — and only once had a losing season.

He won 253 games in his illustrious career. He set a National League record by pitching forty-six and one-third consecutive scoreless innings in 1933 and another by winning twenty consecutive games over the 1936 and 1937 seasons. He was voted into the Hall of Fame in 1947.

Hubbell's most memorable feat came in the second All-Star game, played in New York's Polo Grounds in 1934. Starting for the National League, Hubbell gave up a single to Charley Gehringer and a walk to Heinie Manush in the first inning and prepared to face Babe

In the 1934 All-Star game, King Carl fanned five mighty men in order: Ruth, Gehrig, Foxx, Simmons, Cronin.

Ruth, Lou Gehrig, and Jimmie Foxx, three of the mightiest sluggers in the history of the game.

What followed has often been called by experts the greatest pitching performance in baseball history. Carl Hubbell struck out, in succession, Ruth, Gehrig, Foxx, Al Simmons, and Joe Cronin.

Hubbell pitched his only no-hitter in his second year with the Giants, on May 8, 1929, against the Pittsburgh Pirates. Because it was early in the season and in a game won by the Giants, 11–0, it lacked the importance and drama of some of his other big games.

Carl, himself, never considered the no-hitter his best performance. That came in May of 1940 against the Dodgers. He retired the first sixteen batters he faced before Johnny Hudson hit a ground single. The next man hit into a double play, and Hubbell got the next nine batters in order, facing the minimum twenty-seven men.

"The way I look at it," Hubbell pointed out, "the best game any pitcher can pitch is a game in which he got every batter who faced him — a perfect game. I faced only twenty-seven men against the Dodgers that day. It would have been a perfect game if not for Hudson, but I guess that's what makes a perfect game so rare."

Brother Can You Spare A Hit?

The only similarities between Dizzy Dean and his brother, Paul, were their last name and their ability to throw the high, hard one past hitters.

Dizzy (Jay Hanna Dean) was loud and extroverted, a braggart, a compulsive talker, a great natural wit. Paul was quiet, shy, and introverted. When Dizzy wisecracked, Paul just listened and laughed.

When somebody hung the nickname "Dizzy" on the older of the Dean Brothers, it stuck because it was so descriptive and fitting. When Paul came to the big leagues, somebody tried to tag him with the name "Daffy" as a mate to "Dizzy," but it did not fit Paul's personality.

Because Dizzy was a superior pitcher and a colorful character with an unusual vocabulary and a great sense of humor, Paul remained in the shadow of his older brother. But it was not Dizzy's fault; he constantly tried to promote his brother.

The brothers worshipped one another, and even before Paul joined his brother on the St. Louis Cardinals, Dizzy was touting him. "Old Diz is great," he would say modestly, "but wait 'til you see my brother,

The Dean Boys: Dizzy (left) won 150 games but never a no-hitter; brother Paul won 50 and got his no-hitter.

117

Paul. He's even better. I'm just a sem-eye pro stacked aside of Paul."

Later, when the two were reunited in the big leagues, Dizzy constantly spoke of "Me 'n Paul."

As soon as Paul joined the Cardinals in 1934, Dizzy predicted "Me 'n Paul will win forty or forty-five games between us." They won forty-nine (thirty for Dizzy, nineteen for Paul) and each won two games as the Cardinals defeated the Detroit Tigers in the World Series.

Paul Dean also won nineteen games in his second year, but the following season his arm went dead and he managed to win only twelve games in the next seven years. Ironically, Dizzy's arm went dead a year after Paul's, cutting short two brilliant pitching careers.

Dizzy stayed around long enough to win 150 big-league ball games and to be rated as one of the game's all-time outstanding pitchers, and the last National Leaguer to win thirty games in a season. Paul, unfortunately, won only fifty games in the majors, but there is no telling what he might have achieved had his arm held up.

For all Dizzy's success and Paul's lack of success, the younger brother did something Ol' Diz never did. The Cardinals were playing the Brooklyn Dodgers a double-header in Ebbets Field on September 21, 1934. Dizzy was scheduled to pitch the first game, Paul the second.

The Cards were involved in a torrid race with the New York Giants for the National League pennant and St. Louis manager Frankie Frisch, anxious for a sweep over the lowly Dodgers, called a clubhouse meeting before the double-header to go over the Dodger hitters and warn his players against overconfidence.

Dizzy was unimpressed with the lecture. "I doubt if

them Dodgers will get a hit off either me or Paul today," he boasted to an annoyed Frisch.

Dizzy underestimated the Dodgers. They got three hits in the double-header, all in the first game. In the second game, Paul outdid Dizzy. He pitched a no-hitter! Nobody was more excited about it than Dizzy.

"Now that's real Dean pitchin'," he chirped. "But why didn't you tell me you wuz gonna pitch a no-hitter, Paul, 'cause I'da pitched one, too."

A Change For The Better

Nobody was in awe of the name Bob Lemon in 1948. He pitched for the Cleveland Indians, where the big name was Bob Feller, and fans did not storm the gates because Bob Lemon was pitching against the Detroit Tigers on the night of June 30.

Lemon had won nine games that season, but it was still much too early to take him seriously. After all, he wasn't even a pitcher by preference. Just two years before, Lemon went to spring training with everyone convinced he would take the third-base job away from the aging Ken Keltner. Bob's minor-league record was impressive, but he played poorly that spring and manager Lou Boudreau switched him to the outfield.

Lemon was in center field when the Indians opened the 1946 season and he made a spectacular catch to save the victory for Bob Feller. But it soon became obvious Lemon could not hit big-league pitching, and he was ticketed for return to the minor leagues.

One day Bill Dickey, then manager of the New York Yankees, was talking with Boudreau. "Why don't you try Lemon as a pitcher?" Dickey suggested. "The kid has one of the best curve balls I've ever seen."

While in the army in Hawaii, Lemon had played on the camp baseball team. With the team short of pitchers, Bob volunteered for the job and his work greatly impressed his catcher, Bill Dickey.

Lemon was not overjoyed with Boudreau's suggestion he try pitching. He wanted to play every day, but if this would keep him out of the minor leagues, it was worth a try.

Used exclusively in relief, Lemon won four and lost five and pitched well enough to be given another chance in 1947. He won eleven and lost five and the Indians decided they had themselves an outstanding young pitching prospect. Lemon, however, never abandoned his dream of becoming an every-day player, and stub-

No-hitter of Bob Lemon (center) joined him with mates Don Black (left) and Bob Feller in pitchers' Hall of Fame.

bornly refused to put a pitcher's toeplate on his right shoe.

When the 1948 season started, Lemon was among the pitchers Cleveland's new manager, Al Lopez, was relying on. By June 30 he was taking his regular turn in the rotation, and by July 1 his name would be known all around the country.

For eight innings on that night of June 30, Lemon zipped through the Tigers' batting order without allowing a hit. In the ninth, he retired the first two batters, then faced the dangerous George Kell. The first pitch was five feet wide of the plate, and catcher Jim Hegan went to the mound to try to settle his young pitcher.

"What's the matter, Jim?" Lemon asked with a grin. "Was that last pitch a little wide?"

"I knew then he would be all right," Hegan said.

On the next pitch, Kell hit back to the pitcher and Bob Lemon had pitched the first night no-hitter in the American League.

Three years later, on May 29, 1951, Lemon came close to getting his second no-hitter, also against the Tigers. It was ruined by a home run by Vic Wertz leading off the eighth. He was the only man Bob failed to retire, missing a perfect game by one batter.

Lemon soon became the ace of one of the best pitching staffs ever assembled. From 1949 to 1954 the starting four of Lemon, Feller, Early Wynn, and Mike Garcia won the amazing total of 429 games among them, an average of 17.9 victories per man each season.

When he retired in 1958, Bob Lemon had won 207 big league games — not bad for a fellow who always considered himself an infielder.

SEVEN

ODDLY ENOUGH

The pitch came sailing in to Ray Morgan, the game's first batter, who let it dart by.

"Ball four!" shrieked home plate umpire Brick Owen.

"Whaddya mean, ball?" demanded the pitcher, a burly young left-hander with a cherub's face.

"Get back there and pitch," Owen shouted to the advancing pitcher, "or else you'll be out of here in a minute."

"Yeah," the pitcher said, still advancing, "and if

I'm outta here, you'll get a punch in the nose."

"You're out of here," Owen bellowed, jerking his thumb toward the Boston Red Sox dugout while teammates rushed to restrain the angry, young pitcher.

It was Saturday, June 23, 1917, in Fenway Park, Boston. The Red Sox were meeting the Washington Senators in a double-header and before the first game was two minutes old, the Sox' starting pitcher had been bounced.

Boston manager Jack Barry walked toward the dugout from his position at second base and scanned the men sitting there. Finally, he motioned to a strapping right-hander named Ernie Shore, who had won sixteen games in 1916 and nineteen in 1915.

"Go in there, will you, Ernie," Barry said, "and try to hold them while I get somebody ready."

If he were pitching today, Shore would have been permitted as many warmup pitches as he needed; but in those Spartan days, he was limited to five. What's more, umpire Owen was in no mood to waive the rule.

Shore took his five pitches while two Boston pitchers warmed up hastily in the bullpen. On Shore's first pitch, Morgan streaked for second. Catcher Forrest Cady fired the ball to second, and Morgan was out stealing. Shore retired the next two Washington batters in order.

"How do you feel?" Barry asked after the inning ended. "Shall I get somebody else in there?"

"No," Shore replied. "I'll go on. I'm warmed up now."

Shore went on, mowing down Washington hitters with ease and, when the game ended, he had retired every Washington batter he faced . . . twenty-six up

Ernie Shore got his chance for immortality when Red Sox pitcher Babe Ruth was ejected from a game.

and twenty-six down. It was only the third perfect game in modern baseball history, the first in nine years . . . or was it?

Some skeptics refused to recognize Shore's effort as a no-hitter because he had faced only twenty-six men instead of the minimum twenty-seven. The situation, then and now, has never been specifically covered in the rules. However, he was the pitcher when Morgan was thrown out attempting to steal and the out was credited to Shore's pitching record. On the basis of this, his perfect game has been accepted by the game's historians.

And what ever became of that young, hot-tempered left-hander Ernie Shore had relieved? Shore was traded to the New York Yankees in 1919 and the following year was joined by that same young southpaw, who became bored with pitching and switched to the outfield, where he could play every day instead of every four days.

Playing the outfield for the Yankees, the young man astonished the baseball world by going on a record spree of home-run hitting that was to pump new life into the game of baseball and change the face of the game. In 1920, he slugged fifty-four home runs, almost half the number hit by the entire American League that year. The young ex-pitcher's name? Babe Ruth.

It was thirty-six years after Shore's perfect relief that a young right-hander for the Brooklyn Dodgers named Bob Milliken almost duplicated the feat. Milliken relieved Johnny Podres with two outs in the first inning of a game against the Cincinnati Reds and pitched eight and one-third innings of hitless ball the rest of the way. Podres had wrenched his knee in the first inning, and Milliken came in to retire the side. After walking the first batter in the second inning, he then retired the next twenty-four batters. But he did not gain credit for a no-hitter, nor did he ever come close to matching that performance again.

These days, money alone cannot buy baseball talent. It is a player's market and the only way to acquire a player from another team is to give one of your own in exchange. The successful trader is the fearless trader; the one who will give a good ballplayer to get another player because the latter fills a need; the one who will not worry that the man he trades away will become a star.

Such a man is John Quinn, general manager of the

Philadelphia Phillies. In 1960, the Phillies were in last place, going nowhere fast, when Quinn began a rebuilding program that was to push them toward the top of the National League. One of the things Quinn felt the Phillies needed to achieve success was a second baseman, so he asked the Chicago Cubs if they would part with Tony Taylor. The Cubs said they would if the Phillies would give up Don Cardwell, a hard-throwing right-handed pitcher with outstanding potential who had won nine games for the Phillies in 1959.

The deal was made on May 13. On May 15, Cardwell made his first start in a Chicago uniform and when John Quinn picked up his favorite newspaper at breakfast on the morning of May 16, what he saw did very little for his digestion. Cardwell had pitched a no-hitter for the Cubs in the second game of a double-header and Quinn was a red-faced general manager for the remainder of that season.

But Cardwell's fame was short-lived. He was to be traded two more times in the next six years, while Taylor remained a valuable member of the Phillies for that entire period.

It is ironic that with all the no-hitters that have been pitched, only twice have two been pitched on the same day. One was the famed double no-hitter on May 2, 1917, when Fred Toney of the Cincinnati Reds defeated Hippo Vaughn of the Chicago Cubs, 1–0, in the tenth inning after both had pitched nine hitless innings. The other came before the modern era. On April 22, 1898, Ted Breitenstein of the Cincinnati Reds beat

Baseball's all-time slugger, Babe Ruth, once set a World Series pitching mark for consecutive scoreless innings, 29.

The Reds' Fred Toney
hooked up in rare
pitching duel with
Cubs' Hippo Vaughn.

Vaughn had the mis-
fortune to pick the
wrong day to throw
nine hitless innings.

Pittsburgh for his second no-hitter while James Hughes held Boston hitless for Baltimore.

Then, fifty-eight years later, two no-hitters were almost pitched on the same day again . . . and in the same city.

On Saturday, May 12, 1956, Carl Erskine of the Brooklyn Dodgers took on the New York Giants in Brooklyn's Ebbets Field, while less than ten miles away, Don Ferrarese, a tiny left-hander with the Baltimore Orioles, faced the New York Yankees in Yankee Stadium. With both games being shown on local television, viewers were kept busy trying to follow the action in both games by flipping the dial as Erskine and Ferrarese battled neck and neck, inning after inning, neither pitcher having allowed a hit. Finally, in the ninth, Ferrarese lost his no-hitter when Andy Carey singled. Moments later, Erskine completed the second no-hitter of his career.

Only once did two pitchers from the same team throw no-hitters on consecutive days — in 1917, a boom year for no-hitters. There were seven no-hitters in the majors that year, the most ever pitched in one season.

On May 5, 1917, Ernie Koob of the St. Louis Browns set down the Chicago White Sox in a tainted no-hitter. Koob actually was touched for an infield single in the first inning; but when the game ended with that the only hit off him, the official scorer called a meeting of the writers covering the game and it was agreed to change the hit to an error on the third baseman. That procedure, happily, can no longer occur and the legend that "the first hit in the game should be a good one" has also faded.

The following day, on May 6, Bob Groom followed

Koob's lead and held the White Sox hitless in a 3–0 victory. However, the two no-hitters were not in consecutive games, since Groom's masterpiece came in the second game of a double-header.

The integrity of the game and its players is something of which baseball people are justly proud. Yet, there was one player who tried to help an opponent pitch a no-hitter.

Dazzy Vance, the fabled Brooklyn Dodger flame-thrower, had a no-hitter against Cincinnati with two outs in the ninth inning. The last man he had to get out was Sammy Bohne, a light-hitting infielder, who came to bat carrying a fungo stick, the slim, light, specially constructed bat coaches use to hit fly balls to outfielders during practice. Bohne broke his bat on a Vance high, hard one and the ball looped over shortstop into left field for a single, breaking the no-hitter.

"Preserve me from people trying to do me a favor," Vance moaned. "If Sammy had been mean like most hitters, he'd have used a regulation bat and that would have been an easy fly to left field and I'd have had my no-hitter."

The fates were unkind to Dean Chance of the Minnesota Twins on the night of August 6, 1967. He pitched five perfect innings against the Boston Red Sox — 15 up and 15 down. But a rainstorm halted the game at that point and although he was credited with a 2–0 victory, Chance lost his chance for a no-hitter and baseball immortality.

Dean was to get a second chance. Just 19 days later

Dean Chance did not get credit for a five-inning (rain) no-hitter, but 19 days later it didn't rain.

he faced the Indians in Cleveland, 50 miles away from Wooster, Ohio, where Chance grew up and pitched 18 high school no-hitters. Dean's mother and father and his high school coach were in the stands, and the pitcher was nervous. He walked two batters in the first inning and threw a wild pitch as Cleveland scored a run without a hit.

Then Chance settled down. He held the Indians without a hit for the next eight innings to get the no-hitter he had lost to the rain three weeks earlier. When he returned to the clubhouse a telephone call awaited him. It was from the country's No. 1 Twins' fan, Vice President Hubert Humphrey.

EIGHT

THE LOSERS

The Los Angeles Dodgers of 1965 were a team that got runs like a pair of cast-iron stockings. Their idea of a rally was a walk, a stolen base, an infield out, and a sacrifice fly.

Yet, the Dodgers managed to chug along, scraping and pecking, at a pretty good pace for most of the season because of a couple of miserly pitchers named Don Drysdale and Sandy Koufax. Too often Drysdale and Koufax knew they had to pitch a shutout to win.

One June night, Drysdale lost a 1–0 heartbreaker in

eleven innings. Koufax was scheduled to pitch the following night in Philadelphia, a game that Drysdale was unable to witness. He had been given permission to go to Washington, D.C., on personal business.

When he arrived at his hotel room, Drysdale turned on the radio to find out the baseball scores. He heard the announcer speaking excitedly about Koufax and the no-hitter he had just pitched. He heard the announcer talking about the classic, that it put Sandy in the ranks of the immortals, that he was the first pitcher since Bob Feller to pitch three no-hitters.

It went on like that for several minutes and, finally, Drysdale could stand it no longer and he shouted at the radio: "I don't want to know about history. Tell me, did we win the game?"

The story has been repeated often. It gets a big laugh at banquets, but there is one man who might not think it so funny.

His name is Harvey Haddix and he came to the major leagues in 1952 with the St. Louis Cardinals. For fourteen years, he was one of the most determined, grittiest, most competitive pitchers in baseball. Harvey stood only five feet, nine inches tall and weighed 160 pounds. He never was gifted with the big, overpowering fast ball, but he was long on determination and desire and he had a good head on his shoulders. He was a student of pitching. He knew how to mix up his pitches to keep batters off balance. He battled all the way and had magnificent control of his pitches — he almost always threw the ball in the precise place prescribed by the book on hitters' weaknesses.

In his second full season, Haddix won twenty games for the Cardinals. He also pitched for the Phillies, Reds,

Pirates, and Orioles, finishing up at the age of forty with 136 lifetime victories.

On August 6, 1953, when he was younger and stronger, Haddix had a no-hitter for eight innings pitching against the Philadelphia Phillies. Richie Ashburn, the outstanding slap-hitter, led off the ninth for the Phillies. Catcher Del Rice signaled for a fast ball and Haddix shook his head. He wanted to throw a curve. Ashburn lined it to center for the Phillies' only hit of the game. Poor Harvey had missed his no-hitter. If he had only listened to his catcher!

"I'd throw the same pitch again," Haddix insisted after the game. "I still feel that was the pitch to throw in that spot."

Losing the no-hitter did not matter to Harvey. He won the game and that is what really counted. Besides, Harvey had been disappointed before. When he was with Columbus in the International League, he retired twenty-eight consecutive batters from the second to the eleventh innings after giving up a hit in the first. Harvey knew there would be many more years in front of him. He was sure his chance would come again.

It came in Milwaukee on a muggy, rain-swept May 26, 1959, when he was pitching for the Pittsburgh Pirates. Haddix hooked up in a spectacular pitching duel with tough Lou Burdette. After nine innings, Haddix not only had not allowed a hit, he had not allowed a Brave to reach base . . . twenty-seven up and twenty-seven down. A perfect nine innings, but Harvey could not claim victory because Burdette had held the Pirates scoreless. Several times Pittsburgh came close to scoring, but each time Burdette held them off.

Into the tenth inning they went, all tied up, and

135

again the Braves were unable to get a base-runner and the Pirates were unable to get the run that would make Haddix a winner.

It was the same in the eleventh . . . and in the twelfth. In the thirteenth, Burdette set the Pirates down without scoring and Haddix, weary and frustrated but grimly determined, went out to pitch the last of the thirteenth. The first man up was Felix Mantilla and he lashed a ground ball to third. Don Hoak picked it up, took his time . . . then fired into the dirt in front of first baseman Rocky Nelson and Mantilla was safe, the first Brave to reach base. The spell was broken. But the no-hitter was still alive.

Eddie Mathews sacrificed Mantilla to second and Hank Aaron was walked intentionally. That brought up Joe Adcock. On Haddix' second pitch, Adcock swung and sent a towering drive that disappeared over the right-field wall. Haddix had lost his perfect game, his no-hitter, and the ball game.

It should have been a three-run home run, but in his joy, Aaron cut across the field after touching second base. He was ruled out, Adcock was credited with a double, and the Braves won 1–0.

The score really did not matter. Harvey Haddix had pitched twelve perfect innings, had retired thirty-six men in a row, but lost the game in the thirteenth. It was a crushing defeat, a heartbreaking climax to a brilliant pitching performance.

Reporters descended upon the Pirates' dressing room, which was a tomb of silence. Haddix sat in front of his locker, speaking calmly and philosophically, although the disappointment was visible on his face.

"All I know is that we lost the game," Haddix said.

The Pirates' Harvey Haddix had good reason to feel dejected.

"What's so historic about that? Didn't anyone ever lose a thirteen-inning shutout before?"

One of the reporters told Haddix what was so historic about his game. Never in the history of baseball had a pitcher worked more than ten perfect innings. One had to go all the way back to 1884 to find Edward Kimber of Brooklyn, who pitched ten perfect innings against Toledo. Neither team had scored when darkness ended the game after ten innings.

"Really!" exclaimed Haddix, suddenly aware of the greatness of his accomplishment. "Not even Walter Johnson or Christy Mathewson or Cy Young or some of those great old fellows? Well, what do you know about that!"

There was universal acknowledgement that his was the best-pitched game in history because no one had ever gone so far without permitting a man to get on base. But this was small consolation to Haddix. Next to his name were the words: "Losing pitcher."

"It was just one of those things," he shrugged.

That night Haddix drove Hoak back to the hotel

and the pitcher never mentioned the game or the third baseman's error that broke the perfect streak. It was Hoak who made the only comment.

"I've booted them before and I'll boot them again," he said. That was all. No excuses, no apologies, no vows to make amends in future games that Haddix would pitch.

"That's the kind of guy he is," Haddix explained, "and I admire him for it."

If Haddix was willing to forget his game, baseball would not permit it to be forgotten. National League president, Warren Giles, presented the pitcher with a silver tray and twelve sterling goblets, one for each perfect inning. Engraved on each goblet was the play-by-play account of the Braves' going down in each inning. And, on the tray, was inscribed the following:

TO HARVEY HADDIX
In recognition of his outstanding performance —
unprecedented in baseball history —
Pitching Twelve Consecutive Perfect Innings
Game of May 26, 1959

PITTSBURGH	000 000 000	000	0–0	12	1
MILWAUKEE	000 000 000	000	1–1	1	0

Presented By
National League of Professional Baseball Clubs

It was the first time baseball had made such a presentation, but, then, Harvey Haddix had done something no other player had ever done. However, Haddix was not the first to pitch a full nine innings of no-hit ball and lose — nor would he be the last.

Back on May 9, 1901, Earl L. Moore of Cleveland pitched the first no-hitter in modern times, holding the Chicago White Sox hitless for nine innings. He finally gave up a hit in the tenth and lost the game, 4–2.

Five years later, Harry McIntire of Brooklyn held

the Pittsburgh club without a hit for ten and two-thirds innings, but allowed four hits over the next two and two-thirds innings to lose, 1–0, in thirteen.

There were other hard-luck pitchers over the next few years. Leon Ames of the New York Giants in 1909, Thomas Hughes of the New York Yankees in 1910, and James Scott of the Chicago White Sox in 1914 all pitched at least nine hitless innings and lost.

Then, on the afternoon of May 2, 1917, James (Hippo) Vaughn of the Chicago Cubs and Fred Toney of the Cincinnati Reds hooked up in the greatest pitched game by opposing pitchers in history.

For nine innings neither side made a hit. In fact, no Cincinnati batter had been able to get the ball out of the infield against Vaughn, a left-hander facing a lineup of nine right-handed batters.

In the tenth, with one out, Larry Kopf singled for the Reds against Vaughn. Greasy Neale flied to center fielder Cy Williams for the second out, but Williams muffed Hal Chase's fly, putting runners on second and third. The next batter was the legendary Carlisle Indian, Jim Thorpe. He topped a ball along the third-base line that Vaughn picked up and, realizing he had no chance to nip the speedy Thorpe, fired home. The throw caught catcher Art Wilson by surprise, hitting him on the chest protector, and Kopf scored the game's only run.

Toney completed his no-hitter in the tenth and Vaughn was the loser of baseball's only double no-hit game.

It wasn't until seventeen years and seventeen no-hitters later that Bobo Newsom of the St. Louis Browns lost a game, 2–1, in the tenth after holding the Boston Red Sox hitless for the regulation nine innings.

Topping the list of hard-luck pitchers must be Sam (Toothpick) Jones, who pitched for the Indians, Cubs, Cardinals, and Giants in the 1950's and, with a little bit of luck, might have been the fifth pitcher in history to hurl three no-hitters.

Sam got a no-hitter pitching for the Cubs against the Pittsburgh Pirates on May 12, 1955. Four years later, in a Giant uniform, he beat the Dodgers, 2–0, on a one-hitter . . . a questionable hit at that.

In the eighth inning, Jim Gilliam hit a ground ball to shortstop that Andre Rodgers fielded, then dropped. The official scorer called it a hit, ruling that Gilliam would have beaten the throw even if Rodgers had handled it cleanly. The spectators booed, although the game was played in Los Angeles and Jones was pitching for the hated Giants of San Francisco. Sam thought he had been cheated out of his second no-hitter, and Rodgers insisted it should have been an error, but the decision stayed.

Less than three months later, Jones pitched against the Cardinals and held them hitless for seven innings, when rain came, washing out the remainder of the game. Sam got his victory, but the game would not go into the books as a no-hitter. For a man to receive credit for an official no-hitter, National League president Warren Giles ruled, he must have pitched nine hitless innings.

Ken Johnson pitched the game of his life for the Houston Astros against the Cincinnati Reds on April 23, 1964. He held the Reds without a hit, but became the first pitcher to lose a nine-inning no-hitter when his defense crumbled behind him and the Reds scored a run as a result of two Houston errors in the ninth, the second by the usually sure-handed Nellie Fox at second base.

The following year, the Reds' Jim Maloney had to pitch twenty no-hit innings within nine weeks to get credit for a victory. On June 14, he held the New York Mets hitless for ten innings, but lost in the eleventh when Johnny Lewis slammed a home run. On August 19, he did not allow the Chicago Cubs a hit for ten innings, but this time Maloney's teammates got him a run in the tenth to prevent history from cruelly repeating.

On April 30, 1967, Steve Barber of the Baltimore Orioles became the first pitcher to be knocked out of the box although he had not allowed a hit. Barber, who had walked nine and hit two batters, was one strike from his no-hitter when he threw a wild pitch to Detroit's Mickey Stanley, allowing the tying run to score. When Barber walked Stanley, manager Hank Bauer replaced the pitcher with Stu Miller.

Miller got Don Wert to hit a ground ball to shortstop Luis Aparicio, who threw to second to force Stanley. But second baseman Mark Balanger dropped the ball, and the Tigers scored the winning run without benefit of a hit.

"I didn't deserve a no-hitter," Barber said calmly. "I was too wild."

The situation was similar, but the circumstances more tense for Floyd (Bill) Bevens of the New York Yankees on the afternoon of October 3, 1947. Before a World Series crowd of 33,443 at Brooklyn's Ebbets Field, Bevens, a scatter-armed pitcher of mediocre talents who had won seven and lost thirteen during the regular season, came up to the last of the ninth inning having held the Dodgers hitless.

A no-hitter had never before been pitched in a

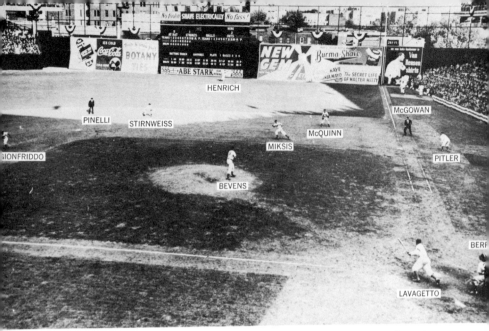

Cookie Lavagetto's drive sails toward the right-field wall and with it goes Bill Bevens' chance for World Series glory.

World Series game, but Bevens' brush with fate was almost overlooked for two reasons. One was the diversion of attention because of the importance placed on the winning or losing of a World Series game. The other was that Bevens' wildness caused people to forget his mastery over Dodger batters. He had walked eight in eight innings and the Dodgers had scored a run in the fifth inning on two walks, a sacrifice, and an infield out.

Every time one looked up, there were Dodgers on base and there was Bevens in hot water, but he still managed to cling to a 2–1 lead into the ninth when, with one out, Carl Furillo walked. When Johnny Jorgensen fouled out, Bevens needed only one more out.

Lavagetto, the Dodger spoiler, attempts to console Yankee Bevens after Cookie's crushing blow.

Al Gionfriddo ran for Furillo and daringly stole second, which made Yankee manager Bucky Harris do something even more daring. He went against the book and ordered Pete Reiser intentionally walked, putting the winning run on base, which is a baseball taboo as old as the game itself.

Eddie Miksis ran for Reiser and the veteran Cookie Lavagetto batted for Eddie Stanky. On Bevens' second pitch, Lavagetto drilled a line drive off the short right-field fence for a double. Gionfriddo scored and so did Miksis. Gone was Bevens' no-hitter and the ball game. A sore arm prevented Bevens from ever again pitching in a major-league game. Nine years later, Don Larsen got revenge in Bevens' behalf by pitching baseball's first World Series no-hitter against the Brooklyn Dodgers.

Heartbreak alley beckoned a young left-hander named Bill Rohr on the afternoon of April 14, 1967. Rohr, three months short of his twenty-second birthday, was pitching for the Boston Red Sox against the Yankees at Yankee Stadium . . . and he was pitching for the first time in a big-league game. After eight innings, he had not allowed a hit and he sent the researchers hustling to the record books.

While Tom Tresh was being retired on a sensational catch by Boston left fielder Carl Yastrzemski, they learned that only eight rookies had ever pitched a no-hitter since the modern era began in 1901. (The ninth rookie proved to be Houston's Don Wilson, the twenty-two-year-old who tossed one in June 1967, against the Braves — the first no-hitter at the Houston Astrodome.)

While Joe Pepitone was popping to right field, they learned that only three pitchers in all the years of base-ball had ever pitched a no-hitter in their first start and that only one, Charles (Bumpus) Jones for Cincinnati in 1892, had ever pitched a no-hitter in his first major-league game.

And just as they were discovering that only three pitchers (Addie Joss of the Cleveland Indians, Mike Fornieles of the Washington Senators, and Juan Marichal of the San Francisco Giants) had pitched one-hitters in their major-league debuts, Elston Howard lashed a line drive to right field to break Bill Rohr's no-hitter and his heart.

There were 14,375 fans in the Stadium that day, most of them avid Yankee fans, but many booed the great Yankee catcher lustily.

"First time in thirteen years I was ever booed for getting a hit," Howard said.

Bill Rohr had learned what it was like to come close to immortality. And Elston Howard had learned what it was like to deprive fans of a chance to witness the rarest of baseball feats.

NINE

BO AND DOUBLE BO

Pitching a no-hitter does not guarantee a man lasting fame, but it does give him instant recognition. It is, in its way, like winning the Irish Sweepstakes. A no-hitter can change a man's life . . . and it has. It changed the life of a journeyman left-hander named Robert Belinsky, better known as Bo.

One day Bo was a twenty-five-year-old rookie who had spent six years knocking around the minor leagues and somehow wound up with the Los Angeles Angels; the next day he was the toast of Hollywood.

146

One day he was a nobody, one of five hundred ballplayers on major-league teams, earning $6,000 a year, and driving around in a year-old Cadillac convertible equipped with push-button windows and a book of installment payments. The next day he was a celebrity pursued by movie stars, newspapermen, and agents and driving around in a year-old Cadillac convertible equipped with push-button windows and no payments remaining.

What happened to Bo Belinsky was not a winning sweepstakes ticket. It was not an inheritance. It was not a lucky night at Las Vegas. What happened to Bo was a no-hitter.

It seems fitting, maybe even preordained, that Belinsky should pitch his no-hitter not in Baltimore, not in Cleveland, not even in New York, but in Los Angeles, so close to Hollywood, the movie capital of the world. There is something unreal about Hollywood. There is also something unreal about Bo Belinsky.

He was born in New York City, but his family moved to Trenton, New Jersey, when Bo was a boy. When he wasn't getting mixed up in street fights, Bo was spending most of his time shooting pool in the local pool hall. He did manage to lay his cue down long enough to pitch in a local recreation league, where he was spotted by the Pittsburgh Pirates and signed for $185 a month. Belinsky was sent to Brunswick, Georgia, which still has not fully recovered from the shock. Brunswick and Belinsky were definitely not made for each other and before the year was out, the city slicker was back in the pool halls of Trenton.

He got another offer, this time to pitch in Pensacola, Florida, which was a little more to Bo's liking. At least he could get a good suntan, something Bo has always treasured.

After winning thirteen, losing six, and striking out 202 batters in 195 innings, his contract was sold to the Baltimore Orioles. Belinsky's itinerary for the next four years of minor-league ball sounds like a Greyhound bus schedule — Knoxville, Aberdeen, Amarillo, Stockton, Pensacola, Vancouver.

Expansion came to the American League in 1961 and, with the need to stock two new teams, talent was scarce. Bo was playing winter ball in Venezuela that winter and doing very well, so the Angels bought his contract from Baltimore for $25,000.

When he checked into the Angels' training camp in Palm Springs, California, nine days late for the start of spring training, 1962, Bo Belinsky was a sight to behold. He walked with a swagger, he dressed cool; and when he spoke, it sounded like he was reading from the script of an old Humphrey Bogart movie. Bo was bold and colorful and tremendously good copy for newspapermen.

The first thing Bo did upon arriving in camp was refuse to sign his contract, which called for $6,000 and a $1,000 increase if he made the team. The $6,000 was all right, but he wanted to keep the renegotiation open figuring that by June 15 he would be in a position to demand more than $1,000.

"Look," he was told firmly, "you either sign this contract or take the next plane back to Trenton."

He signed.

The whole thing was almost academic. Bo took a consistent pounding all through spring training, but the Angels refused to give up on him and took him to Los Angeles to open the season. Two things weighed heavily in Belinsky's favor. First, the Angels had made a considerable investment in him. Second, he had what they call in the trade "a major-league arm." That is, he could throw hard and his ball moved. He had only to learn control and the intelligence of pitching and he could be a success.

When Angels' manager Bill Rigney started him against the Kansas City Athletics on April 19, it seemed Bo was pitching for his baseball life — and it seemed that life was slipping away.

He walked the first man he faced, gave up a double to the second, walked the third, and was tagged for a single by the fourth. Two runs were in, two men on base and nobody out in the first inning. Belinsky had one foot in the baseball graveyard.

He proceeded to strike out the next batter and five of the eight batters that followed. He pitched six innings, then had to retire because of a blister and wound up the winning pitcher in a 3–2 game.

He pitched a complete game against Cleveland in his next start, then won his third straight game, going six innings against the Indians.

Then it was the night of May 5 in Los Angeles' Dodger Stadium and Bo was scheduled to pitch against the Baltimore Orioles, the team that sold him to Los Angeles. There were 15,886 in the stands, a crowd so small that Belinsky was insulted. More than that, he had revenge on his mind as he faced the Orioles.

The Angels scored a run in the first and another in the second off Steve Barber, an old Oriole minor-league teammate of Belinsky's. Meanwhile, the Orioles could not do a thing against Bo except get bases on balls. He walked four men in nine innings and struck out nine, but

Pals Bo Belinsky (left) and Dean Chance had many things in common, including no-hitters.

not one ball was hit hard against him. And when the ninth inning was over, Bo Belinsky had pitched a no-hitter. With the final out, Los Angeles fans showered the field with seat cushions. He was the second rookie to pitch a no-hitter in modern times.

Manager Bill Rigney was one of the first to greet Belinsky. "How was that for a rookie?" Bo asked brashly.

Belinsky's post-game press conference was something else. "It couldn't happen to a nicer team," he said, needling the Orioles. "I'm not going to ask for more money," he promised. "I'll just wait and let them come and insist I take a raise."

Hollywood flipped for Bo Belinsky as only Hollywood can. He got his name in the columns and movie stars accepted him and wanted to be with him. He became part of the chic set. Like Batman, Belinsky was an overnight sensation, and other overnight sensations of other years welcomed him to their world of Hollywood glamour. His picture was in the papers constantly. He was greeted as a celebrity in all the hip places and he began to date famous movie stars like Ann-Margret and Mamie Van Doren.

Belinsky made the most of his new-found world. He talked of going to acting school and becoming a motion-picture star. He had all kinds of deals in the fire and he mingled with Hollywood's most famous stars. All because of a no-hitter.

Belinsky was the talk of the town and he continued to be as he won two more games and showed a 6–0 record after the first six weeks of the season.

Then the big, gay bubble burst. For the remainder of the season he won only four and lost eleven. The following year, he was 2–9 when the Angels shipped him to Hawaii and, after the 1964 season, the Angels traded him to the Philadelphia Phillies. Later, he landed with the Houston Astros.

In his first five big-league seasons he averaged five victories a season. Each of his teams kept hoping he would again find the skill that had enabled him to pitch a no-hitter.

Bo may never find it, but at least it has been an enjoyable ride on the baseball roller coaster. Belinsky had had fun and he had been around the big leagues long enough and won enough games to prove that he is not another Bobo Holloman, as many predicted he would be.

Alva (Bobo) Holloman had spent nearly a decade in the minor leagues when he came to the St. Louis Browns. In 1952, he had a record of 16–7 at Syracuse in the International League. When he won two games in the Puerto Rico World Series in winter ball following the 1952 season, Bill Veeck, general manager of the pathetic Browns, decided to take a chance on Bobo. The price was cheap enough — $10,000 — plus an additional $25,000 if Bobo survived the June 15 deadline for trimming team rosters.

Veeck was a good judge of baseball talent, but he had never seen Holloman pitch. Still, the reports were good and his record was, too, and Veeck figured he had to be worth $10,000. Bill was never so wrong in his life.

Bobo, to put it politely, was something of a character. When the Browns purchased his contract, they sent him a questionnaire, routine procedure with most clubs when they acquire a new player. One of the questions was: "Do you have any superstitions?"

"Yeah," replied Holloman. "I write the initials of my wife and kid in the foul lines before I pitch. ALWAYS." The capital letters were Bobo's.

"Any big moments?" was another query.

"Sure. I've pitched five one-hitters. And once I pitched a one-hitter and won my own game with a home run. I did that on July 4 because that's my kid's birthday."

Bobo had acquired his nickname from Bobo Newsom, a zany character who spanned four decades of pitching in the major leagues.

Like Belinsky, Holloman was discovered playing winter ball and like Belinsky, Holloman was late reporting to spring training in 1953.

It soon became obvious to Veeck that he had made a terrible mistake in purchasing Holloman. One look at him convinced Veeck of that. Survive the June 15 cutdown? Bobo would be lucky if he survived batting practice. He couldn't strike out his own grandmother.

"He could outtalk me, outcon me, and outpester me," Veeck wrote in his book, *Veeck As In Wreck*, "but he couldn't outpitch me. In spring training he was hit harder trying to get batters out than our batting practice pitchers who were trying to let them hit."

The only thing that consoled Veeck was the thought that he would not have to shell out the additional $25,000 to keep Holloman past June 15.

When the season started, Bobo was used in a few relief assignments by manager Marty Marion with the expected results. Bobo complained loud and clear. "I'm a starting pitcher," he protested, "not a relief pitcher. Give me a starting shot and I'll show you what I can do.

He pestered Marion every day for a month and

when he got nowhere, he took his case to Veeck, who listened with a sympathetic ear. Finally, Veeck decided to tell Marion to let Holloman have his shot. What better way to dispose of him for once and for all?

Bobo was named to pitch against the powerful New York Yankees, which Veeck knew was like tossing him to a bunch of hungry lions. But, just as he was ready to pitch to lead-off batter Phil Rizzuto, there was a cloudburst and a rainstorm fell that forced cancellation of the game.

Perhaps Veeck felt sorry for poor Bobo because his next start, on May 6, was against the Philadelphia Athletics, the softest competition in the league. Bobo etched an "N" for Nan and a "G" for Gary in the foul line and went out to pitch. Again, there was a cloudburst, but the intermittent rain was not heavy enough to call the game.

Bobo pitched, and everything he threw was belted and everywhere the ball went, there was a Brownie to catch it. It was like a miracle taking place. Billy Hunter was an acrobat at shortstop. Jim Dyck spent most of the night climbing the left-field wall to pull down long drives and Roy Sievers made three incredible plays at first base.

Because the night was hot and humid and the air was damp and heavy, drives that seemed headed out of the park were held up and caught at the fences. And just when Bobo appeared to be tiring, a shower would sweep across the field delaying the game long enough for him to rest and come back refreshed.

It went on like this for nine innings. Fantastic catches; drives curving foul at the last moment; hard line drives hit right into fielders' gloves. And when it was all over, Bobo Holloman had a no-hitter and Bill Veeck had

When the Browns' Bobo Holloman got the opportunity, he made the most of it.

an expensive problem.

Bobo had become the first pitcher in baseball's modern era to pitch a no-hitter in his first major-league start. Suddenly Bobo was an immortal and not even Bill Veeck would dream of sending an immortal to the minor leagues, so he was stuck with him past the June 15 cutdown date.

Bobo's no-hitter was the first for the St. Louis Browns in nineteen years and the first winning one for the Browns in thirty-six years, to the day. It was also the last no-hitter pitched for the St. Louis Browns, because the following year they moved out of St. Louis and became the Baltimore Orioles.

But when they did, Bobo Holloman was not around to make the move with them. He had pitched a few more times and won two games, but he had never pitched another complete game. On July 23, Bobo was sold to Toronto, never to be heard from in the major leagues again. The price for Bobo's contract was $7,500, representing a $27,500 loss for Veeck.

Perhaps it is a disservice to Louis (Bobo) Newsom

155

to mention him in the same breath with Alva (Bobo) Holloman. They are linked only by their nicknames and by the fact that each pitched a no-hitter.

In an unusual career that began in 1929 and ended in 1953, Newsom won 208 more games than Holloman. Newsom also lost 222 games, but he was a valuable pitcher who pitched for nine different teams, had two twenty-win seasons, won two World Series games for Detroit against Cincinnati in 1940, and won his last major-league game at the age of forty-six.

Because of double and triple hitches with several teams, no pitcher in the history of baseball moved around as much as old Bobo. He changed teams sixteen times, and it was often suspected that Bobo tried a little harder against the teams to which he hoped to be traded.

Considering his zany career, it seemed fitting that itinerant Bobo Newsom's no-hitter should have an unhappy ending.

There was never anyone more colorful in baseball than Bobo Newsom, a robust 225-pound right-hander who was extremely tough in close ball games. In 1938, he won twenty games for the seventh-place St. Louis Browns, but his biggest year came in 1940 with the Detroit Tigers.

He won twenty-one and lost five to lead the Tigers to the American League pennant. With his father in the stands, Bobo beat the Reds in the first game of the 1940 World Series, 7–2. That night his dad had a heart attack and died the next morning. Scheduled to pitch the fifth game, Bobo decided to go through with the assignment.

"Dad would have wanted me to," he said and went out and blanked the Reds, 8–0, on a three-hitter. When Cincinnati tied the Series at three games apiece, Newsom was called on to pitch the seventh game with just one day's rest. He held the Reds scoreless for six innings, then gave up two runs in the seventh and lost the game, 2–1.

It is unfortunate for all his good work on the mound that Bobo should be best remembered as one of baseball's zaniest characters, which he was.

In 1936, he started the opening game for Washington against the Yankees with President Franklin Delano Roosevelt in the stands. In the fourth inning, Ben Chapman bunted the ball to third base, where it was picked up by the Senators' third baseman, Ossie Bluege, who fired to first. Bobo forgot to duck and the ball struck him flush on the jaw.

He wobbled off the field, was administered to by the Washington trainer, then returned to complete the game and beat the Yankees, 1–0, pitching with a broken jaw.

President Franklin Delano Roosevelt came to throw out the first ball in 1936, and Bobo Newsom didn't disappoint him.

"When the President comes to see Bobo pitch," he said later, "ol' Bobo ain't a gonna disappoint him."

Once he boasted that he had found a way to stop Joe DiMaggio, the great Yankee Clipper. That afternoon, Joe banged three doubles off Bobo.

"See that," Newsom said proudly, "Bobo found his weakness. It's the two-base hit. He got no homers off Bobo."

On September 18, 1934, Bobo took the mound for the Browns against the Boston Red Sox. The Browns picked up an early run and the Red Sox tied the game a few innings later, but they could not get a hit off Bobo — for nine innings. He had a nine-inning no-hitter!

The score was tied, 1–1, and the game had to go into extra innings. In the tenth Bobo finally gave up a hit — and lost the game, 2–1.

It could only have happened to Bobo.

TEN

HEX MARKS THE SPOT

Sandy Koufax kicked high, around came his left arm, and the ball was a blur as it buzzed past the New York Mets' Felix Mantilla and exploded into the mitt of catcher John Roseboro for strike three.

It was the night of June 30, 1962, in Los Angeles' Dodger Stadium and the magnificent left-hander had just breezed through the first inning with the greatest of ease. He threw nine pitches and struck out three Mets.

As Sandy walked off the mound and headed for the Los Angeles dugout, his path crossed that of Met third-base coach, Solly Hemus.

"You know something?" Hemus said. "You've got a no-hitter."

What Hemus was trying to do was upset Koufax by invoking a superstition almost as old as the game itself. The superstition contends that if anyone mentions a no-hitter while the game is in progress, the no-hitter will be broken.

So Hemus mentioned it . . . and mentioned it . . . and mentioned it. After every inning, when their paths crossed, he reminded Sandy Koufax of the no-hitter he was pitching. After every inning, that is, except the ninth. By then he didn't have to say a word. The roar of the crowd said it for him because Sandy Koufax had pitched the first of his four no-hitters.

Because Hemus defied the superstition and Koufax still got his no-hitter, one might think that would clear up, once and for all, the notion that one can jinx a no-hitter by mentioning it. It didn't. Ballplayers still cling to their individual idiosyncrasies while a no-hit game is in progress, although many pitchers scoff at the superstition.

In 1951, while the Yankees' Allie Reynolds was in the process of throwing the first of his two no-hitters, he shouted from the mound to catcher Yogi Berra, "Mix 'em up more. You want one of these fellows to guess what's coming and maybe ruin our no-hitter?"

During his perfect game against the Mets in 1964, Jim Bunning of the Philadelphia Phillies talked about it constantly.

"He was chattering away like a magpie," remembered catcher Gus Triandos.

After each inning, Bunning would go to the Phillies' bench and say, "Only nine more outs to go, do something out there . . . only six more outs to go, dive for the ball . . . only three more outs and I've got it."

"I think," said Phillie manager Gene Mauch, "he did that as much to relax his teammates as himself."

During the fifth game of the 1956 World Series as Don Larsen set down the Brooklyn Dodgers in order inning after inning, it was so quiet in the Yankee dugout you could hear the grass grow in the infield. After he had set the Dodgers down for the seventh consecutive inning, Larsen came into the dugout to the customary greeting of dead silence. Larsen broke the silence, addressing Mickey Mantle.

"Hey, Mick," he said. "I've got only two more innings to go to make it. Say a prayer for me, will you?"

Mantle looked shocked. Without a word he got up and walked to the other end of the dugout as if to say, "Let me get away from this crazy guy before he puts a jinx on himself."

On the surface, the silent treatment would seem to be a silly, senseless ritual. The first man in the ball park to know there is a no-hitter in progress is the pitcher who is pitching it, if he is concentrating on the game.

And if he should lose his concentration, it is right up there on the scoreboard for all to see — pitcher included — or he will notice the change of attitude on the bench or the tension in the stands as the crowd becomes aware of history in the making and cheers each out. And, if all else fails to penetrate, some killjoy on the other team is certain to remind him what he has accomplished in the hope of distracting him as Hemus attempted to distract Koufax.

Nobody knows for certain how the superstition got

started. It probably occurred when a player mentioned a no-hitter on the bench and seconds later it was broken. Baseball players being the superstitious lot they are, the player was no doubt censured for jinxing the pitcher, and the tradition was born. Now, during a no-hitter, they not only remain silent, many make certain to sit on the same seat next to the same player in the dugout every inning, let the same player lead them out on the field, and go through the same mannerisms so as not to disturb the routine.

While on the field players are performing their own rituals, upstairs in the broadcasting booth strange things may also be happening.

To mention a no-hitter or not to mention a no-hitter? That is the problem that has plagued radio and television broadcasters for decades because inevitably their mail tells them they are wrong if they do and they are wrong if they don't.

Most announcers have enrolled in the school of thought which says their job is to inform listeners what is going on, a policy probably established by Red Barber, veteran announcer for the Cincinnati Reds, Brooklyn Dodgers, and New York Yankees.

"In 1935, I was selected as one of the announcers to

Veteran sportscaster
Red Barber took a
bold position in
describing no-hitters.

broadcast the World Series," Red recalls. "Commissioner Landis called us together and I'll never forget his words. He said, 'Gentlemen, your job is to report what you see, not to editorialize.' I've always tried to follow that advice and that goes for no-hitters, too."

The policy caused the mailman to work overtime when Red made frequent reference to the no-hitter the Yankees' Bill Bevens was pitching in the fourth game of the 1947 World Series. Cookie Lavagetto of the Brooklyn Dodgers eventually broke the spell with two outs in the ninth.

"A lot of people wanted to string me up on the nearest tree," Barber recalls. "But I always felt I had no right to ignore hits . . . even the absence of hits . . . just as I had no right to ignore errors or runs. I consider that to be the single broadcast I'm proudest of because right then, I feel I matured as a broadcaster."

Red Barber has broadcast about a dozen no-hitters and one that stands out in his mind is Tex Carleton's for Brooklyn against Cincinnati in 1940. Broadcasters did

Everybody celebrated Tex Carleton's no-hitter. That's Leo Durocher sitting between Tex (right) and Herman Franks.

Sportscaster Mel Allen believed in following dugout tradition in regard to no-hitters.

not travel with the club in those days and Red did a re-creation of the game in a studio from the play-by-play sent by Western Union ticker.

"There were two outs in the ninth," Barber recalls, "and the ticker flashed an out and, I'll never forget it, I said, 'I don't know how he made out, but he's out and it's a no-hitter!'"

Another veteran announcer, Mel Allen, for years the "Voice of the New York Yankees," differed in his approach to a no-hitter.

"I always believed in simply following the tradition of the dugout," he explained. "The tradition of not mentioning a no-hitter was not started by broadcasters, but was carried over from the dugout.

"All you do is avoid saying 'he's pitching a no-hitter.' There are ways of saying it without using those words. You can say 'team Y has had only one man reach base and that was on a walk.' Or, 'only six outs remain between Allie Reynolds and immortality.' When television came along, it was easier because the camera would show the scoreboard and you could call attention of the viewers to the totals on the scoreboard. You're just being respectful of the dugout tradition, but you still get mail."

Bob Wolff, who formerly broadcast the Washington Senator and Minnesota Twins games, called Don Larsen's perfect game and handled the problem in this manner:

"Your first obligation is to be an honest reporter. But you have to recognize your obligation to all fans, even the minority of fans who are superstitious, and to flaunt their superstitions is to needlessly incur their wrath. With the Larsen game, I tried to mention it innocuously and without ostentation. There are several ways to do this without mentioning the words 'no-hitter.' You can say, 'all six batters up have gone down in a row.' Or, 'as you look across the Dodger totals on the scoreboard, they are completely blank.'

"The thing that gets people angry is if a man makes a hit the moment after you mention 'no-hitter.' So you separate the mention of no-hitter, if you must mention it, from the immediacy of a hit. That is, you say it after the pitcher has completed an inning and there are at least ten minutes before the hitless team comes to bat again and, by then, people will have forgotten you mentioned it. I am proud to say that in the Larsen game, I did not receive one letter from a fan who accused me of jinxing Larsen or one who thought I did not let him know what was going on in the game."

For almost ten years, Pat Harmon, a Cincinnati newspaperman, conducted a one-man campaign to get pitcher-turned-radio-announcer Waite Hoyt to mention the words "no-hitter." Hoyt continued to cling to his ballfield superstition and refused to mention it, until his mail indicated fans wanted it after Jim Maloney pitched ten hitless innings against the Mets in 1965.

In 1959, while Harvey Haddix was pitching twelve perfect innings, Pittsburgh Pirate announcer Bob Prince deftly danced around the words "no-hitter" and "perfect game." Among other things, after three innings he said, "first nine men up and down." In the sixth, he announced, "Haddix has zeroed the board."

In the eighth, he warned, "Don't go away, we're on the verge of . . . baseball history." After Haddix had completed nine perfect innings, Prince screamed "Harvey Haddix has pitched a perfect no-hit, no-run game." Then he lost his voice.

"I believe in telling the people," says another ex-player, Joe Garagiola, who announced the New York Yankee games with two other ex-players, Phil Rizzuto and Jerry Coleman. "In fact, I'll try to build up the audience by saying, 'if you've got any friends not listening, call them up. We might have a no-hitter here tonight.' "

It is Garagiola's contention that the pitcher is the first to know. "The scoreboard is there, the mood is going to change, or the bench jockeys are going to get on him. If he's a young pitcher, they'll say, 'Hey, you're too young to pitch a no-hitter.' "

Garagiola recalls once when he was playing, Ralph Branca of the Brooklyn Dodgers had a no-hitter going against his Pittsburgh Pirates. "Before every inning, we kept yelling at him, 'Here goes your no-hitter.' We practically had the Norman Luboff choir going for us."

Bob Elson, who has called nine no-hitters in almost four decades as the voice of the Chicago White Sox, says he believes in telling his listeners when a no-hitter is in progress, and his mail indicates the fans want it that way.

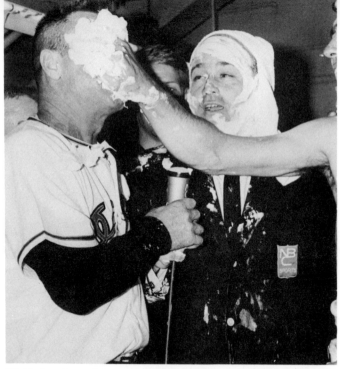

NBC's Joe Garagiola, a clubhouse cut-up and former ballplayer, gets serious on the subject of no-hitters.

"Certainly I mention it," says Harry Caray, who does the St. Louis Cardinals' games. "You've got to report what's happening. You don't think twice about doing it, you just do it."

Caray can recall only one no-hitter involving the Cardinals in his years at the microphone. "We never had one pitched for us in my time and there was only one pitched against us. Don't forget, we had a fellow named Stan Musial around here for a long time."

Not only does Vince Scully, voice of the Los Angeles Dodgers, call no-hitters, but if it gets late in the game and the pitcher is from the Los Angeles area, he'll say, "If you know his folks, tell them to tune in. Their boy is pitching a no-hitter."

Scully says it is a tribute to fans that they no longer

complain that a broadcaster is jinxing a pitcher by mentioning a no-hitter. "People don't want you to insult their intelligence. They don't believe you're sticking pins in dolls."

Scully, who may be the only man to have called two perfect games (Larsen's and Koufax') says he never had any doubt how he would call a no-hitter when he was a rookie announcer. He broke in under Red Barber in Brooklyn and Barber said call it, so Scully called it.

"The players mention it themselves these days," Vince says. "I remember Roger Craig coming into the dugout after six or seven hitless innings, shouting, 'Hey, I've got a no-hitter.'"

One game that stands out vividly in Scully's memory came on June 19, 1952, in Chicago. Carl Erskine, scheduled to pitch for Brooklyn that day, was sitting in the dugout, flipping a baseball into the air, when Scully sat down next to him.

"I wonder," Erskine said, "what this little baseball has in store for me today."

That day Erskine pitched the second no-hitter of his career.

In recent years Scully has instituted something new in broadcasting. If a pitcher has a no-hitter for eight innings, he will call his studio and have an engineer tape the ninth inning. Making certain to mention the date sometime during the inning, Scully will then present the tape to the pitcher as a memento if he gets his no-hitter.

After Sandy Koufax had pitched three no-hitters and received three tapes and was in the process of pitching his fourth, Scully said to himself, "What else can I do for Sandy to make this tape different?"

"I decided to give the time of day after each out," he remembers. "I would say, 'It's 9:49 and Koufax is two outs away from a no-hitter!' People tell me it had a very dramatic effect."

When the New York Mets came into existence in 1962 and hired Lindsey Nelson, Bob Murphy, and Ralph Kiner as their air men, the trio sat down to discuss policy. One of the things they discussed was the calling of a no-hitter and they agreed to mention it.

"On the basis of simply reporting a ball game," Nelson says, "you must tell people what is happening. People are tuning in and out all the time and unless you tell them, they might miss it. Also, we owe it to our sponsors to keep people tuned in."

When Koufax pitched his no-hitter against the Mets in 1962, Nelson stayed with his policy of mentioning the no-hitter and got a barrage of telegrams.

"How can you do that?" was the tenor of the telegrams. "How can you try to jinx the no-hitter?"

So, Nelson had Koufax as a guest on the pre-game show the next day and asked Sandy if he believed announcers should mention a no-hitter.

"Why not?" replied Sandy. "We mention it on the field all the time. Roseboro came out in the seventh inning and said, 'Don't walk this man, but don't forget you've got a no-hitter, so don't make the pitch too good.'"

That convinced Lindsey Nelson he was doing the right thing and from that moment he has laughed off any criticism he gets on the subject.

"I figure," he maintains, "if anything I say in the broadcasting booth can influence anything going on down on the field, I ought to be getting more money."

ELEVEN

PERFECT

As man and boy, there had been nothing special in the life of Don Larsen. No silver spoon was in his mouth when Donald James Larsen came into the world in Michigan City, Indiana, on August 7, 1929. As an infant, he did not pick up his rattle and throw a perfect strike into the hands of his pediatrician.

Failure and frustration had highlighted a major-league career that dates back to 1953. In that time, he won eighty-one big-league games and lost ninety-one for seven teams, a record that does not qualify him for induction into baseball's Hall of Fame, nor does it explain how and why Don Larsen was chosen for one special moment. Perhaps it is this air of mystery surrounding him that made Larsen's achievement all the more incredible.

As a boy, Don did not show any overwhelming interest in baseball until his family moved to San Diego, California, when he was fifteen. Even then, at Point Loma High School, he got more recognition as a hitter than as a pitcher. This ability to hit was to carry over to his major-league career, and Casey Stengel would one day speculate that Don might have been a $40,000 ballplayer as an outfielder.

Don's mother recalls that she never gave any thought to her son's becoming a professional ballplayer.

"Don didn't seem to have any special talent for the game," she remembers. "He played the outfield sometime, but he never cared for it. He did like to pitch, though, and always seemed happiest when he was in the middle of the action."

It was while pitching American Legion ball that Don began to show some potential, enough to interest Art Swartz, a scout for the St. Louis Browns, who was impressed by Don's strong throwing arm. The Browns signed him in 1947 and sent him to Aberdeen in the Northern League.

With the exception of 1948, when he won seventeen and lost eleven, Larsen's minor-league career was less than distinguished. After four minor-league seasons, his career was interrupted by two years in military service; and when he was discharged in 1953, he joined the rag-tag Browns, a team in desperate need of pitchers.

In his first year he showed a 7-12 record for a team

171

that finished last and lost 100 games. Opinion was divided on the big, hard-throwing right-hander, but Satchel Paige, the ageless veteran of what seemed like a century in the Negro leagues, was a teammate of Larsen's and quickly tabbed him a future star.

"A little more experience is what he needs," Satch predicted. "Then look out. He's gonna win twenty, twenty-five games one year and don't forget, ol' Satch told you."

Don never fulfilled ol' Satch's prediction. With a year under his belt, he should have improved. Instead, he got worse. In 1954, when the Browns became the Baltimore Orioles, he won only three and lost twenty-one, the most in the league. But two of his victories were against the New York Yankees, who saw something in the big guy that appealed to them. That winter, the Yankees and Orioles engineered a seventeen-man trade, biggest in baseball history. The key man for the Yankees was Bob Turley, a flame-throwing right-hander who had won fourteen games for the seventh-place Orioles. Almost overlooked in the enormous deal was the fact that Don Larsen also went to New York. The Yankees had insisted on big Don's inclusion in the swap and the Orioles agreed, almost matter-of-factly.

Pitching for a pennant-contending team, one that could score runs by the barrel, should have helped Larsen's record. But by May 11, he had won one and lost one and the Yankees sent him to Denver. The demotion was designed to teach Larsen a lesson, get him to work harder and to gain a greater appreciation for life in the major leagues. It succeeded. His work in Denver merited Larsen's return on July 31 and he went on to win eight out of nine games and help the Yankees win the American League pennant.

Awarded a starting assignment in the fourth game of the World Series, Don was shelled unmercifully by the Brooklyn Dodgers, who clubbed him for five runs in four innings. He never got back into the Series, which was won by the Dodgers in seven games.

The Yankees expected 1956 would be a big year for Larsen, but he was kayoed in five of his first seven starts and his record was a disappointing 7-5 by September. However, he finished the season by winning four straight to end up with a respectable 11-5 record. In his last game against the Red Sox, after the Yankees had already clinched the pennant, Don tried something new. Suspecting he was tipping off his pitches to the opposition, he experimented pitching without a windup. He simply brought the ball to his belt buckle, bent at the waist, kicked, and threw. It was an unorthodox delivery, but it worked.

Because of Don's strong finish, manager Casey Stengel named Larsen as his pitcher for the second game of the 1956 World Series against the Dodgers. Don was eager to avenge his humiliation of the previous year. Perhaps he was too eager.

The Yankees jumped off to a 6–0 lead, scoring one in the first and five in the second and, as he went out to pitch the last of the second, Larsen thought he could practically coast home a winner. But when he walked four batters in the inning, Stengel came out to replace him with Johnny Kucks.

"When Casey came to take the ball away from me he was mad," Don recalls. "That made two of us because I was mad, too. I was mad at myself, Casey, the Dodgers — everybody in the world. I was still boiling in the

173

clubhouse. I figured I had blown my chance. I was sure I'd never get another chance to start in that Series."

But Don was wrong. After the Yankees won the fourth game to tie the Series at two games apiece, there was a great deal of speculation as to the identity of the Yankee pitcher for the important fifth game. If the Yankees lost that game, they would be hard pressed to win the Series, since the scene would shift to Brooklyn's Ebbets Field for the last two games and the power-hitting Dodgers were practically invincible in their tiny ball park. To add to the odds, the Dodgers' fifth-game pitcher was to be the crafty veteran, Sal Maglie, who had stifled the Yankees in game number one.

Stengel's long-awaited announcement of his fifth-game pitcher came as a surprise to the press. "Larsen," the old man growled, then hastened to explain his choice. "He wasn't throwin' in Brooklyn, he was just pushin' the ball up there. Maybe he was worried about the fences. He can pitch better. You'll see."

The night before his big chance, Larsen had a quiet dinner with friends, including a New York sportswriter. Shortly after midnight, they hopped a cab and headed for Larsen's hotel.

"I'm gonna beat those guys tomorrow," Don suddenly blurted, "and I'm just liable to pitch a no-hitter, too."

"A four-hitter should be good enough," the writer said. It was a private joke. Earlier that season, when Larsen was 7-5, he told the same sportswriter, "I'm gonna pitch four four-hitters in the next four games." (He pitched three four-hitters and one three-hitter.)

"No," Larsen insisted. "I feel I've got a no-hitter in me."

When the alarm rang at eight the next morning, Don hated to get up. He liked to sleep late, but the game was scheduled to start at 1 P.M. and Stengel liked his players to check into the clubhouse three hours before game time. Never much of a breakfast eater, Don had only a cup of tea. A friend came by to pick him up and as the two men rode to Yankee Stadium in a taxi, Larsen was still in a grumpy mood.

"How do you feel?" asked the friend.

"I feel mad enough to be a winner," Larsen growled.

When he arrived at the Stadium, he changed from his street clothes into his uniform. Pete Previte, one of the Yankees' clubhouse men, brought him a can of fruit juice. He was still not hungry and declined food. He surprised himself with his calmness. It was almost an hour to game time and he was still not nervous.

When it was forty minutes before game time, Don walked out to take his preliminary warmup pitches. He threw lightly to catcher Charlie Silvera, then feeling the muscles in his arm loosen in the warmth of the noon-day sun, he began throwing harder. It was then that Larsen's disposition began to brighten. He was hitting Silvera's target consistently and his breaking stuff was sharper than usual.

He felt good all of a sudden. For the first time he began to appreciate what a nice day it was. "How nice it is to be pitching in big Yankee Stadium," he thought.

It wasn't until he walked to the mound for the first inning that Larsen felt a touch of nervousness. He looked up into the packed stands. There were 64,519 in the huge Stadium that Monday, October 8, and Larsen could feel the butterflies in his stomach; but he was

175

certain they would disappear once he had thrown his first pitch.

After three innings, Larsen knew he would have to pitch an outstanding game to win. Neither he nor Maglie had allowed a hit for three innings and Don knew Maglie was going to be particularly tough. The veteran curve baller, a fierce competitor, was baseball's comeback story of the year. Picked up by the Dodgers from Cleveland in May, Sal had gone on to win thirteen games, capping his season with his first no-hitter at the age of thirty-nine, just thirteen days before.

In the fourth, Mickey Mantle broke the spell by slamming a Maglie delivery into the right-field seats for the first hit of the game. Larsen made the lead stand up and, with the help of several outstanding defensive plays, he did not allow a hit through six innings.

In the second, Jackie Robinson had lashed a drive to third that bounced off Andy Carey's glove into the hands of shortstop Gil McDougald, who threw Jackie out at first. In the fifth, Gil Hodges had slammed a drive to left

With the Yankees and Dodgers tied at two games each in the 1956 World Series, Don Larsen was a surprise starter.

The last pitch of the fifth game of the 1956 World Series was the biggest one for Larsen.

center that Mickey Mantle caught with a running, back-handed catch. In the same inning, Sandy Amoros' line drive screamed into the right-field stands, foul by no more than a foot.

The Yankees picked up another run in the sixth to ease the pressure on Larsen. But the real pressure was yet to come.

Don made it three up and three down for the seventh consecutive inning, and in the eighth, the pressure grew unbearable and the crowd was cheering on every pitch. By the time Larsen went out to start the ninth, one could cut the tension with a knife. The crowd gasped with each pitch as Larsen got Carl Furillo to fly to right field and Roy Campanella to ground to second. One batter to get and there was a hush in the stands as Dale Mitchell, swinging two bats, slowly walked to the plate to pinch-hit for Maglie.

Larsen turned toward center field and raised his

head to the sky. "Help me out, somebody," he said silently. "Please help me out."

In center field, Mickey Mantle said a silent prayer. "Please don't let them hit the ball to me."

In the Yankee bullpen in right field, pitcher Rip Coleman, Larsen's roommate, turned away from the field, afraid to look.

The first pitch to Mitchell was a ball and Don thought, "Oh, no. All day I've been getting ahead of the hitters and now I have to get behind on the last batter."

The next pitch was a strike and so was the next. "That's more like it," Don thought.

He took off his cap and wiped the perspiration that was on the cap against his left knee. He fired a fast ball and Mitchell swung viciously and the ball went spinning back against the backstop. Foul ball.

"Just got under it," Larsen thought. "A half inch higher and that's a line drive."

On the next pitch, Larsen put all of his 220 pounds into a fast ball. Mitchell started to swing, then held and Babe Pinelli shot his right hand into the air. It was all over. There was bedlam. Yogi Berra dashed to the mound and leaped on the pitcher-hero and soon players and fans were swarming all around him, carrying him off the field. The roar of the crowd was a crescendo, and there were tears of joy in the eyes of many in the crowd because of the enormity of it all.

In the dressing room, reporters gathered around him and Larsen was still visibly shaken with emotion. He trembled as he tried to light a cigarette.

"I don't believe it happened to me, I don't believe it. I'm shaking like a leaf. I can't think. How can I answer questions? I still can't believe it," Larsen kept

178

Catcher Yogi Berra, previously on the receiving end of no-hitters, never caught a more exciting one.

saying over and over.

"When it was over, I was so happy, I felt like crying. I wanted to win this one for Casey. After what I did in Brooklyn, he could have forgotten about me and who would blame him? But he gave me another chance and I'm grateful."

For ninety minutes, Don sat answering questions. He answered the same questions dozens of times as new waves of reporters came to him.

"I was nervous . . . I prayed . . . the pressure was murder . . . I did it for Casey . . . I was so happy I could have . . ."

From time to time, the interview was interrupted when special well-wishers came by to shake his hand. There were Dan Topping and Del Webb, owners of the Yankees, and baseball commissioner Ford C. Frick; and, in a display of sportsmanship, the Dodgers' Jackie Robinson and Sal Maglie came by to add their congratulations to a fellow professional.

Maglie was a gracious loser. "I felt sorry for you in the ninth, Don," the dark bearded Maglie said, "because I knew what was going through your mind. You were the best and there was nothing we could do about it."

The Yankee Stadium switchboard recorded 2,217 calls for Larsen that day. The mayor of Michigan City, Indiana, Larsen's birthplace, named a street after him. Of the thousands of letters and telegrams that poured in, the one that gave him the biggest thrill read as follows:

> Dear Mr. Larsen:
>
> It is a noteworthy event when anybody achieves perfection in anything. It has been so long since anyone pitched a perfect big-league game that I have to go back to my generation of ballplayers to recall such a thing — and that is truly a long time ago.
>
> This note brings you my very sincere congratulations on a memorable feat, one that will inspire pitchers for a long time to come. With best wishes.
>
> Sincerely,
> Dwight D. Eisenhower
> President of the United States

The months that followed were a whirlwind of excitement for the perfect pitcher. There were personal appearances, television shows, parties, magazine interviews, banquets, awards.

Don Larsen was sitting on top of the world. Three years later, he was traded to Kansas City. He bounced around the major leagues after that and by 1966, he was back in the minor leagues.

It is one of the sad stories of baseball that Don Larsen, the perfect pitcher, was never the same again. In the nine years following his epic performance, he won only forty-one games and people shook their heads sadly whenever his name was mentioned.

Perhaps too much was expected of him after the perfect game. Perhaps he would have been better off if he never had pitched that game — a game he could not possibly duplicate. Don Larsen never went along with this kind of thinking. He lived a lifetime in those nine innings. For one day, for ninety-seven pitches, for two hours and six minutes on an October day in 1956, he was the greatest pitcher who ever lived. That was something that could not be taken away from him. He never complained about the bad times that followed.

As the years passed, he treasured the thrill of that one day and he remembered, with a chuckle, the sportswriter who struck Casey Stengel speechless.

"Did Larsen ever pitch a greater game?" the sportswriter asked.

The end of a perfect day: Casey Stengel and Don Larsen.

COMPLETE LIST OF NO-HIT GAMES

(From the *Little Red Book of Baseball*, compiled by the Elias Sports Bureau)

1875   Joseph Borden, Philadelphia vs. Chicago, NA, July 28 .. 4–0
1876   George Washington Bradley, St. Louis vs. Hartford,
      NL, July 15 2–0
1880   *John Lee Richmond, Worcester vs. Cleveland,
      NL, June 12 1–0
      *John Montgomery Ward, Providence vs. Buffalo,
      NL, June 17 5–0
      Lawrence Corcoran, Chicago vs. Boston, NL, Aug. 19.. 6–0
      James Galvin, Buffalo vs. Worcester, NL, Aug. 20 1–0
1882   Anthony Mullane, Louisville vs. Cincinnati, AA,
      Sept. 11 2–0
      Guy Hecker, Louisville vs. Pittsburgh, AA, Sept. 19 ... 3–1
      Lawrence Corcoran, Chicago vs. Worcester, NL,
      Sept. 20 5–0
1883   Charles Radbourne, Providence vs. Cleveland, NL,
      July 25 8–0
      Hugh Dailey, Cleveland vs. Philadelphia, NL,
      Sept. 13 1–0
1884   Albert Atkisson, Philadelphia vs. Pittsburgh, AA,
      May 24 10–1
      Edward Morris, Columbus vs. Pittsburgh, AA,
      May 29 5–0
      Frank Mountain, Columbus vs. Washington, AA,
      June 5 12–0
      Lawrence Corcoran, Chicago vs. Providence, NL,
      June 27 6–0
      James Galvin, Buffalo vs. Detroit, NL, Aug. 4 18–0
      Richard Burns, Cincinnati vs. Kansas City, UA,
      Aug. 26 3–1
      Edward Cushman, Milwaukee vs. Washington, UA,
      Sept. 28 5–0
      Edward Kimber, Brooklyn vs. Toledo, AA, Oct. 4
      (ten innings) 0–0
1885   John Clarkson, Chicago vs. Providence, NL, July 27 ... 4–0
      Charles Ferguson, Philadelphia vs. Providence, NL,
      Aug. 29 1–0
1886   Albert Atkisson, Philadelphia vs. New York, AA,
      May 1 3–2
      William Terry, Brooklyn vs. St. Louis, AA, July 24 1–0
      Matthew Kilroy, Baltimore vs. Pittsburgh, AA, Oct. 6.. 6–0

1888	William Terry, Brooklyn vs. Louisville, AA, May 27 ..	4–0
	Henry Porter, Kansas City vs. Baltimore, AA, June 6 ..	4–0
	Edward Seward, Philadelphia vs. Cincinnati, AA, July 26	12–2
	August Weyhing, Philadelphia vs. Kansas City, AA, July 31	4–0
1890	Ledell Titcomb, Rochester vs. Syracuse, AA, Sept. 15..	7–0
1891	Thomas Lovett, Brooklyn vs. New York, NL, June 22..	4–0
	Amos Rusie, New York vs. Brooklyn, NL, July 31	6–0
	**Theodore Breitenstein, St. Louis vs. Louisville, AA, Oct. 4	8–0
1892	John Stivetts, Boston vs. Brooklyn, NL, Aug. 6	11–0
	Alex Sanders, Louisville vs. Baltimore, NL, Aug. 22 ...	6–2
	**Charles Jones, Cincinnati vs. Pittsburgh, NL, Oct. 15	7–1
1893	William Hawke, Baltimore vs. Washington, NL, Aug. 16	5–0
1897	Denton (Cy) Young, Cleveland vs. Cincinnati, NL, Sept. 18	6–0
1898	Theodore Breitenstein, Cincinnati vs. Pittsburgh, NL, April 22	11–0
	James Hughes, Baltimore vs. Boston, NL, April 22	8–0
	Frank Donohue, Philadelphia vs. Boston, NL, July 8 ..	5–0
	Walter Thornton, Chicago vs. Brooklyn, NL, Aug. 21..	2–0
1899	Charles Phillippe, Louisville vs. New York, NL, May 25	7–0
	Victor Willis, Boston vs. Washington, NL, Aug. 7	7–1
1900	Frank Hahn, Cincinnati vs. Philadelphia, NL, July 12..	4–0
1901	Earl Moore, Cleveland vs. Chicago, AL, May 9 (Lost in 10)	2–4
	Christopher Mathewson, New York vs. St. Louis, NL, July 15	5–0
1902	James Callahan, Chicago vs. Detroit, AL, Sept. 20	3–0
1903	Charles Fraser, Philadelphia vs. Chicago, NL, Sept. 18..	10–0
1904	*Denton (Cy) Young, Boston vs. Philadelphia, AL, May 5	3–0
	Robert Wicker, Chicago vs. N.Y., NL, June 11 (Gave hit in 10th)	1–0
	Jesse Tannehill, Boston vs. Chicago, AL, Aug. 17	6–0
1905	Christopher Mathewson, New York vs. Chicago, NL, June 13	1–0
	Weldon Henley, Philadelphia vs. St. Louis, AL, July 22	6–0
	Frank Smith, Chicago vs. Detroit, AL, Sept. 6	15–0
	William Dineen, Boston vs. Chicago, AL, Sept. 27 ...	2–0
1906	John Lush, Philadelphia vs. Brooklyn, NL, May 1	1–0
	Malcolm Eason, Brooklyn vs. St. Louis, NL, July 20 ..	2–0
	Harry McIntire, Brooklyn vs. Pitt., NL, Aug. 1 (Lost in 13)	0–1

1907	Frank Pfeffer, Boston vs. Cincinnati, NL, May 8	6–0
	Nicholas Maddox, Pittsburgh vs. Brooklyn, NL, Sept. 20	2–1
1908	Denton (Cy) Young, Boston vs. New York, AL, June 30	8–0
	George Wiltse, N.Y. vs. Phil., NL, July 4 (10 innings)..	1–0
	George Rucker, Brooklyn vs. Boston, NL, Sept. 5	6–0
	Robert Rhoades, Cleveland vs. Boston, AL, Sept. 18 ..	2–1
	Frank Smith, Chicago vs. Philadelphia, AL, Sept. 20 ..	1–0
	*Adrian Joss, Cleveland vs. Chicago, AL, Oct. 2	1–0
1909	Leon Ames, New York vs. Brooklyn, NL, April 15 (Lost in 13)	0–3
1910	Adrian Joss, Cleveland vs. Chicago, AL, April 20	1–0
	Charles Bender, Philadelphia vs. Cleveland, AL, May 12	4–0
	Thomas Hughes, New York vs. Cleveland, AL, Aug. 30 (Gave hit in 10th)	0–5
1911	Joseph Wood, Boston vs. St. Louis, AL, July 29	5–0
	Edward Walsh, Chicago vs. Boston, AL, Aug. 27	5–0
1912	George Mullin, Detroit vs. St. Louis, AL, July 4	7–0
	Earl Hamilton, St. Louis vs. Detroit, AL, Aug. 30	5–1
	Charles Tesreau, New York vs. Philadelphia, NL, Sept. 6	3–0
1914	James Scott, Chicago vs. Washington, AL, May 14 (Lost in 10)	0–1
	Joseph Benz, Chicago vs. Cleveland, AL, May 31	6–1
	George Davis, Boston vs. Philadelphia, NL, Sept. 9 ...	7–0
	Edward LaFitte, Brooklyn vs. Kansas City, FL, Sept. 19	6–2
1915	Richard Marquard, New York vs. Brooklyn, NL, April 15	2–0
	Frank Allen, Pittsburgh vs. St. Louis, FL, April 24 ..	2–0
	Claude Hendrix, Chicago vs. Pittsburgh, FL, May 15..	10–0
	Miles Main, Kansas City vs. Buffalo, FL, Aug. 16	5–0
	James Lavender, Chicago vs. New York, NL, Aug. 31..	2–0
	Arthur Davenport, St. Louis vs. Chicago, FL, Sept. 7..	3–0
1916	Thomas Hughes, Boston vs. Pittsburgh, NL, June 16 ..	2–0
	George Foster, Boston vs. New York, AL, June 21 ...	2–0
	Leslie Bush, Philadelphia vs. Cleveland, AL, Aug. 26..	5–0
	Hubert Leonard, Boston vs. St. Louis, AL, Aug. 30 ..	4–0
1917	Edward Cicotte, Chicago vs. St. Louis, AL, April 14..	11–0
	George Mogridge, New York vs. Boston, AL, April 24	2–1
	Fred Toney, Cincinnati vs. Chicago, NL, May 2 (10 innings)	1–0
	James Vaughn, Chicago vs. Cincinnati, NL, May 2, (Lost in 10)	0–1
	Ernest Koob, St. Louis vs. Chicago, AL, May 5	1–0

	Robert Groom, St. Louis vs. Chicago, AL, May 6	3–0
	*Ernest Shore, Boston vs. Washington, AL, June 23 ..	4–0
1918	Hubert Leonard, Boston vs. Detroit, AL, June 3	5–0
1919	Horace Eller, Cincinnati vs. St. Louis, NL, May 11 ..	6–0
	Raymond Caldwell, Cleveland vs. New York, AL, Sept. 10	3–0
1920	Walter Johnson, Washington vs. Boston, AL, July 1 ..	1–0
1922	*Charles Robertson, Chicago vs. Detroit, AL, April 30	2–0
	Jesse Barnes, New York vs. Philadelphia, NL, May 7 ..	6–0
1923	Samuel Jones, New York vs. Philadelphia, AL, Sept. 4..	2–0
	Howard Ehmke, Boston vs. Philadelphia, AL, Sept. 7..	4–0
1924	Jesse Haines, St. Louis vs. Boston, NL, July 17	5–0
1925	Arthur (Dazzy) Vance, Brooklyn vs. Philadelphia, NL, Sept. 13	10–1
1926	Theodore Lyons, Chicago vs. Boston, AL, Aug. 21	6–0
1929	Carl Hubbell, New York vs. Pittsburgh, NL, May 8 ...11–0	
1931	Wesley Ferrell, Cleveland vs. St. Louis, AL, April 29 ..	9–0
	Robert Burke, Washington vs. Boston, AL, Aug. 8 5–0	
1934	Louis Newsom, St. Louis vs. Boston, AL, Sept. 18 (Lost in 10)	1–2
	Paul Dean, St. Louis vs. Brooklyn, NL, Sept. 21	3–0
1935	Vernon Kennedy, Chicago vs. Cleveland, AL, Aug. 31..	5–0
1937	William Dietrich, Chicago vs. St. Louis, AL, June 1 ..	8–0
1938	John Vander Meer, Cincinnati vs. Boston, NL, June 11	3–0
	John Vander Meer, Cincinnati vs. Brooklyn, NL, June 15	6–0
	Monte Pearson, New York vs. Cleveland, AL, Aug. 27..13–0	
1940	Robert Feller, Cleveland vs. Chicago, AL, April 16 ...	1–0
	James Carleton, Brooklyn vs. Cincinnati, NL, April 30	3–0
1941	Lonnie Warneke, St. Louis vs. Cincinnati, NL, Aug. 30	2–0
1944	James Tobin, Boston vs. Brooklyn, NL, April 27	2–0
	Clyde Shoun, Cincinnati vs. Boston, NL, May 15	1–0
1945	Richard Fowler, Philadelphia vs. St. Louis, AL, Sept. 9..	1–0
1946	Edward Head, Brooklyn vs. Boston, NL, April 23	5–0
	Robert Feller, Cleveland vs. New York, AL, April 30 ..	1–0
1947	Ewell Blackwell, Cincinnati vs. Boston, NL, June 18 ..	6–0
	Donald Black, Cleveland vs. Philadelphia, AL, July 10..	3–0
	William McCahan, Philadelphia vs. Washington, AL, Sept. 3	3–0
1948	Robert Lemon, Cleveland vs. Detroit, AL, June 30 ...	2–0
	Rex Barney, Brooklyn vs. New York, NL, Sept. 9	2–0
1950	Vernon Bickford, Boston vs. Brooklyn, NL, Aug. 11 ..	7–0
1951	Clifford Chambers, Pittsburgh vs. Boston, NL, May 6..	3–0
	Robert Feller, Cleveland vs. Detroit, AL, July 1	2–1

	Allie Reynolds, New York vs. Cleveland, AL, July 12 ..	1–0
	Allie Reynolds, New York vs. Boston, AL, Sept. 28 ...	8–0
1952	Carl Erskine, Brooklyn vs. Chicago, NL, June 19	5–0
	Virgil Trucks, Detroit vs. Washington, AL, May 15 ..	1–0
	Virgil Trucks, Detroit vs. New York, AL, Aug. 25	1–0
1953	**Alva (Bobo) Holloman, St. Louis vs. Philadelphia, AL, May 6	6–0
1954	James Wilson, Milwaukee vs. Philadelphia, NL, June 12	2–0
1955	Samuel Jones, Chicago vs. Pittsburgh, NL, May 12 ..	4–0
1956	Carl Erskine, Brooklyn vs. New York, NL, May 12 ..	3–0
	Melvin Parnell, Boston vs. Chicago, AL, July 14	4–0
	Salvatore Maglie, Brooklyn vs. Philadelphia, NL, Sept. 25	5–0
	***Donald Larsen, New York, AL, vs. Brooklyn, NL, Oct. 8	2–0
1957	Robert Keegan, Chicago vs. Washington, AL, Aug. 20..	6–0
1958	James Bunning, Detroit vs. Boston, AL, July 20	3–0
	Hoyt Wilhelm, Baltimore vs. New York, AL, Sept. 20..	1–0
1959	Harvey Haddix, Jr., Pittsburgh vs. Milwaukee, NL, May 26 (Pitched 12 perfect innings, allowed hit in 13, lost)	0–1
1960	Donald Cardwell, Chicago vs. St. Louis, NL, May 15 ..	4–0
	Lou Burdette, Milwaukee vs. Philadelphia, NL, Aug. 18	1–0
	Warren Spahn, Milwaukee vs. Philadelphia, NL, Sept. 16	4–0
1961	Warren Spahn, Milwaukee vs. San Francisco, NL, April 28	1–0
1962	Robert (Bo) Belinsky, Los Angeles vs. Baltimore, AL, May 5	2–0
	Earl Wilson, Boston vs. Los Angeles, AL, June 26	2–0
	Sanford (Sandy) Koufax, Los Angeles vs. New York, NL, June 30	5–0
	William Monbouquette, Boston vs. Chicago, AL, Aug. 1	1–0
	John Kralick, Minnesota vs. Kansas City, AL, Aug. 26	1–0
1963	Sanford (Sandy) Koufax, Los Angeles vs. San Francisco, NL, May 11	8–0
	Donald Nottebart, Houston vs. Philadelphia, NL, May 17	4–1
	Juan Marichal, San Francisco vs. Houston, NL, June 15	1–0
1964	Kenneth Johnson, Houston vs. Cincinnati, NL, April 23 (Lost)	0–1
	Sanford (Sandy) Koufax, Los Angeles vs. Philadelphia, NL, June 4	3–0
	*James Bunning, Philadelphia vs. New York, NL, June 21	6–0

1965 James Maloney, Cincinnati vs. New York, NL, June 14
   (10 innings, gave two hits in 11th, lost) 0–1
  James Maloney, Cincinnati vs. Chicago, NL, Aug. 19
   (10 innings) 1–0
  *Sanford (Sandy) Koufax, Los Angeles vs. Chicago,
   NL, Sept. 9 1–0
  David Morehead, Boston vs. Cleveland, AL, Sept. 16 .. 2–0
1966 Wilfred (Sonny) Siebert, Jr., Cleveland vs. Washington, AL, June 10 2–0
1967 Don Wilson, Houston vs. Atlanta, NL, June 18 2–0
  Dean Chance, Minnesota vs. Cleveland, AL, Aug. 25 .. 2–1
  Joe Horlen, Chicago vs. Detroit, AL, Sept. 10 6–0
1968 Tom Phoebus, Baltimore vs. Boston, AL, April 27 6–0

NA—National Association   UA—Union Association
NL—National League   FL—Federal League
AA—American Association   AL—American League

*—Perfect game
**—First major-league start
***—World Series (perfect game)

INDEX

A

Aaron, Hank, 136
Adcock, Joe, 136
Alexander, Grover Cleveland, 13, 50, 52
Allen, Lee, 36–37
Allen, Mel, 164–165
Allen, Richie, 30
Alston, Walter, 25, 103
Altman, George, 49
Amalfitano, Joey, 32
Ames, Leon, 139
Amoros, Sandy, 177
Aparicio, Luis, 141
Appling, Luke, 89
Ashburn, Richie, 25–27, 135

B

Banks, Ernie, 32
Barber, Red, 162–164, 168
Barber, Steve, 141
Barry, Jack, 123
Bauer, Hank, 141
Behrman, Hank, 75
Belanger, Mark, 141
Belinsky, Robert (Bo), 146–149, 151–152, 153
Berra, Yogi, 11, 54–55, 160, 178
Bevens, Floyd (Bill), 91, 92, 141–142, 144, 163
Blackwell, Ewell, 72–76
Blanchard, Doc, 72
Bluege, Ossie, 157
Bohne, Sammy, 130
Borden, Joseph Emley (Josephs, Joseph Emley), 36–37
Boudreau, Lou, 92, 119–120
Bradley, George Washington, 35–36, 41
Branca, Ralph, 166
Breitenstein, Ted, 38–39, 127, 129

Browne, Byron, 32
Bunning, Jim, 46–49, 160–161
Burdette, Lou, 45, 98–100, 135–136

C

Cady, Forrest, 123
Camilli, Dolph, 69–70
Campanella, Roy, 22, 59, 177
Campanis, Al, 19
Campbell, Bruce, 81–82
Caray, Harry, 166–167
Cardenas, Leo, 62, 64
Cardwell, Don, 127
Carey, Andy, 129, 176
Carey, Max, 66
Carleton, Tex, 163
Caylor, Oliver Perry, 37
Chambers, Cliff, 13
Chapman, Ben, 157
Chance, Dean, 130, 132
Chase, Hal, 139
Christopher, Joe, 48
Cobb, Ty, 52
Coleman, Rip, 178
Collins, Rip, 84
Corcoran, Lawrence J., 30, 38, 93–94
Craft, Harry, 70–71, 77
Craig, Roger, 168
Cronin, Joe, 116

D

Dalrymple, Clay, 98
Daniel, Dan, 56–57
Dark, Alvin, 61
Davis, Glenn, 72
Dean, Jay Hanna (Dizzy), 13, 82, 84, 86, 88, 116–119
Dean, Paul, 116–119
Derringer, Paul, 68
Dickey, Bill, 91, 92, 119–120
DiMaggio, Joe, 9, 12, 56, 90–91, 92, 158

189

Drebinger, John, 56–58
Driscoll, Dave, 66
Drysdale, Don, 32, 133–134
Durocher, Leo, 70, 77, 82, 84
Dyck, Jim, 154

E

Eisenhower, President Dwight D., 180
Elson, Bob, 166
Erskine, Carl, 22, 59–62, 129, 168
Etten, Nick, 91

F

Feller, Robert, W. A. (Bob), 23, 30, 42, 50, 53, 78–94, 119, 121, 134
Feller, William (father of Bob), 79–81, 85
Ferrarese, Don, 129
Fletcher, Art, 113
Ford, Whitey, 13
Fornieles, Mike, 145
Foster, Phil, 59
Fox, Nellie, 140
Foxx, Jimmie, 114, 116
Frick, Commissioner Ford C., 180
Frisch, Frank, 82, 118
Furillo, Carl, 22, 59, 142, 144, 177

G

Galan, Augie, 75
Gallatin, Harry, 16
Galvin, James F., 38
Garagiola, Joe, 166
Garcia, Mike, 121
Garibaldi, Art, 84
Gehrig, Lou, 9, 114, 116
Gehringer, Charley, 114
Giles, Warren, 137, 140
Gilliam, Jim, 140
Gionfriddo, Al, 144
Gomez, Lefty, 9
Gonder, Jesse, 46–47, 48
Gordon, Joe, 56, 91
Griffith, Clark, 107–108
Grimes, Burleigh, 70
Grissom, Lee, 68
Gromek, Steve, 56
Groom, Bob, 130
Grove, Lefty, 13, 50

H

Haddix, Harvey, 134–138, 166
Haney, Fred, 100
Harmon, Pat, 165
Harris, Bucky, 107, 144
Hassett, Buddy, 69
Hayes, Frankie, 92
Head, Ed, 13, 58
Hegan, Jim, 121
Hemus, Solly, 159–160, 161
Hendley, Bob, 32
Henrich, Tommy, 90–91, 92
Hermanski, Gene, 75
Heydler, John, 66
Hickman, Jim, 48
Hoak, Don, 136, 137–138
Hodges, Gil, 21, 59, 61, 178
Holloman, Alva (Bobo), 13, 152-156
Holmes, Ducky, 67
Hooper, Harry, 107
Howard, Elston, 134
Hoyt, Waite, 165
Hubbell, Carl, 113–114, 116
Hudson, Johnny, 116
Hughes, James, 129
Hughes, Thomas, 139
Humphrey, Vice President Hubert, 132
Hunt, Ron, 48
Hunter, Billy, 154

J

Johnson, Ken, 140
Johnson, Lou, 32
Johnson, Walter, 49, 89, 106–108
Jones, Charles (Bumpus), 37, 145
Jones, Sam (Toothpick), 140
Jorgensen, Johnny, 142
Joss, Addie, 145

K

Kanehl, Rod, 25–26
Keegan, Bob, 13
Kell, George, 121
Keller, Charlie, 91, 92
Keltner, Ken, 119
Kerlan, Dr. Robert, 30, 31
Kieran, John, 50

Kimber, Edward, 137
Kiner, Ralph, 169
Kinsella, Edward, 113–114
Koob, Ernie, 12, 129–130
Kopf, Larry, 139
Koufax, Sanford (Sandy), 12, 14, 15–34, 38, 42, 48, 49, 60, 94, 133–134, 159–160, 161, 168, 169
Koy, Ernie, 70
Kranepool, Ed, 48
Krug, Chris, 32
Kucks, Johnny, 173
Kuenn, Harvey, 32

L

Labine, Clem, 103
Landis, Commissioner Kenesaw Mountain, 163
Landrum, Don, 62
Larsen, Don, 10–11, 14, 103, 144, 161, 165, 168, 170–181
Laurie, Milt, 18
Lavagetto, Cookie, 69, 144, 163
Lemon, Bob, 119–121
Lewis, Johnny, 63, 141
Lombardi, Ernie, 70
Lopez, Al, 121

M

Mack, Connie, 50
Mack, Ray, 89, 92
MacPhail, Larry, 67, 68, 71
Maglie, Sal, 10, 100–103, 174, 176–177, 180
Maloney, Jim, 62–64, 141, 165
Mantilla, Felix, 25–27, 135, 159
Mantle, Mickey, 60, 161, 176–178
Manush, Heinie, 114
Marichal, Juan, 95–98, 145
Marion, Marty, 153, 154
Maris, Roger, 11
Marquard, Rube, 109–110
Martin, Pepper, 82, 84
Martin, Stu, 82, 84
Mathewson, Christy, 11, 41, 50–53
Matthews, Eddie, 136
Mauch, Gene, 161
McCahan, Bill, 13

McCovey, Willie, 95
McDougald, Gil, 176
McGraw, John, 50, 113–114
McIntire, Harry, 138–139
McKechnie, Bill, 67–68, 70
Medwick, Joe, 82
Miksis, Eddie, 144
Miller, Eddie, 75
Miller, Stu, 141
Milliken, Bob, 125
Mitchell, Dale, 11, 177
Moore, Earl L., 41, 138
Moore, Terry, 82, 84
Morgan, Ray, 122, 123, 124
Morris, Edward, 38
Mountain, Frank T., 38
Murphy, Bob, 169
Murphy, Jimmy, 18–19
Musial, Stan, 167

N

Neale, Greasy, 139
Nelson, Lindsey, 169
Nelson, Rocky, 136
Newcombe, Don, 22
Newsom, Louis (Bobo), 139, 153, 156–158

O

Ogrodowski, Bruce, 82
O'Neill, Steve, 82, 84
Owen, Brick, 122–123

P

Paige, Satchel, 172
Pepitone, Joe, 144
Pesky, Johnny, 56, 58
Phelps, Babe, 69
Pinelli, Babe, 11, 178
Plank, Eddie, 13, 106
Podres, Johnny, 125
Prince, Bob, 166

Q

Quinn, John, 125, 127

R

Ramsdell, Willard, 60
Reese, PeeWee, 22, 59, 73
Reiser, Pete, 144
Reynolds, Allie (Wahoo), 53–58, 160

Rice, Del, 135
Rice, Grantland, 52–53
Richards, Paul, 105–106
Richmond, John Lee, 37
Riggs, Lew, 70
Rigney, Bill, 97–98, 149
Rizzuto, Phil, 56–57, 90, 91, 154
Roberts, Robin, 13
Robinson, Jackie, 22, 59, 75–76, 176, 180
Robinson, Wilbert, 111
Rodgers, Andre, 140
Rohr, Bill, 144–145
Rojas, Cookie, 48
Roosevelt, President Franklin D., 157, 158
Rosen, Goody, 70
Ruffing, Red, 10
Rusie, Amos, 51
Ruth, Babe, 9, 50, 52, 108, 114, 116, 125

S

Sain, Johnny, 45, 93, 100
Samuel, Amado, 49
Santo, Ron, 32
Schang, Wally, 85
Scott, James, 139
Scully, Vince, 167–169
Shaute, Joe, 66, 67
Shawkey, Bob, 85
Sherry, Norm, 24–25
Shore, Ernie, 123–125
Sievers, Roy, 154
Silvera, Charlie, 175
Simmons, Al, 116
Sisler, Dick, 31
Slapnicka, Cy, 79, 80–81, 82
Smith, Edgar, 88
Smith, Gov. Alfred E., 113–114
Smith, Red, 46
Snider, Duke, 22, 59
Spahn, Warren, 43–46, 50
Stanky, Eddie, 75, 144
Stanley, Mickey, 141
Stengel, Casey, 45, 171, 173, 174, 175, 181
Sturdivant, Tom, 49

Stephenson, Johnny, 49
Stirnweiss, George, 90, 91, 92
Sullivan, Billy, 88
Swartz, Al, 171

T

Taft, President William Howard, 106–107
Taylor, Tony, 47, 48, 127
Thomson, Bobby, 11
Thorpe, Jim, 139
Toney, Fred, 127, 139
Topping, Dan, 180
Tresh, Tom, 144
Triandos, Gus, 48, 49, 106, 160
Trucks, Virgil (Fire), 56–58
Turley, Bob, 172

V

Vance, Arthur Charles (Dazzy), 110–111, 113, 130
Vander Meer, Johnny, 53, 65–71, 73, 74, 76, 77
Vaughn, James (Hippo), 127, 139
Veeck, Bill, 152, 153, 154–155

W

Waddell, Rube, 109
Walters, Bucky, 68
Ward, John Montgomery, 37–38
Webb, Del, 180
Wert, Don, 141
Wertz, Vic, 58, 121
Wilhem, Hoyt, 103–106
Williams, Ted, 54–55
Williams, Cy, 139
Wills, Maury, 12
Wilson, Art, 139
Wilson, Don, 144
Wolff, Bob, 165
Woodling, Gene, 53
Wright, Taft, 89
Wynn, Early, 13, 121

Y

Yastrzemski, Carl, 144
Young, Denton True (Cy), 30, 39, 41, 49, 93, 103

Z

Zientara, Benny, 75